Invitation to Intimacy

By Fount Shults

Invitation to Intimacy: Reflections on the Lost and Found Parables

Publisher: Patrick Selvey

ISBN: 978-0-9992334-6-7

Invitation to Intimacy was previously published in 2011. This version was revised and expanded in 2021.

All Scripture quotations are the author's own — which are influenced by the Revised Standard Version. Copyright © 1952, 1971 Zondervan Bible Publishers.

Fount Shults has been married to his wife, best friend, and partner in ministry, Lynda, since 1964. They have six children, 12 grandchildren and two great grandchildren. Together they founded *On Word Ministries* in 1987.

Fount is available for speaking engagements. For further information please visit www.onword.org or write to fount@onword.org

Dedicated to all my former students

Table of Contents

Introduction

The parable of the prodigal son has been an inspiration to Christian men and women throughout the centuries. It speaks of a father and two sons. The younger son intentionally shamed his father, left home and later returned. The older son worked hard in the field to win his father's approval but would not celebrate his brother's return from the foreign country.

This collection of reflections will focus mostly on the father and his unconditional love for both sons. He represents our Father in heaven and his love for the world. The sons represent two ways of responding to the Father's love. The elder brother has a performance orientation, as though one must earn love. The younger stands for those who spurn Abba's affection and try to find fulfillment in things and experiences.

The younger brother also represents the journey back into the father's embrace. The nature of that return trip will be another major focus of these meditations. His return began when *"he came to himself."* We will try to unpack the meaning of that phrase looking for insight to help us move forward in our own journey into our Father's bosom.

The purpose of this introduction is to prepare the reader to gain the most from these meditations as they unfold. Like a road map, this will acquaint the reader with the journey before it begins. The first thing you will notice on the 'map' is that we must travel through the parables of the lost sheep and the lost coin before we have the clues to understanding the Prodigal. Hopefully, you, the reader, will be able to recognize yourself in the reflections and advance in your personal journey as you read and think on these things.

Look for your Father God in the unfolding drama and allow your heart to respond honestly and freely. Your heart will not lead you into a dangerous place, although it might lead you to recognize things you usually try to hide from yourself. Abba's embrace is waiting on the other side of this self-recognition.

A Farmer and Four Sons

The parable speaks of a father and two sons. However, as we look more closely, we will discover four sons present. The elder brother and the prodigal are obvious. We often overlook the Son who is telling the story. He is the third son - the Son of our Father in heaven. He is the first Son in priority.

Jesus is the Son of Love who came to this foreign country to reveal Father's nature to sinners (the prodigals). He also came to the religious 'field' to invite the Pharisees (the elder brothers) to receive Father's free grace. Jesus came into the world (to the foreign land and to the field) not to condemn and exclude the sons of Adam (humanity), but to invite them back to intimacy (Jn. 3:17). That is the main point of the parable: "Come home."

In Luke 15 Jesus told two other parables of lost things. His primary audience for all three was the Pharisees who were critical of him because he ate with sinners. They were despising those whom Jesus loved. He hoped they would recognize themselves as elder brothers. Jesus wanted them to stop trying to earn Abba's free favor and just receive it.

Many of the Pharisees did recognize themselves in the story. Some of them rejected his invitation to intimacy and became angry with the Son who was telling the story. Others, like Nicodemus, eventually responded openly to his appeal. Still others remained secret disciples (Jn. 19:38).

The sinners probably recognized themselves in the story as younger brothers. They had already begun their journey back to Father's house because Jesus was offering Abba's loving embrace without demanding they change first. They were comfortable in the presence of the Son because he accepted them as they were. The Son was also comfortable with them.

So, there are the two brothers in the parable itself, and the third is Jesus the Son of Father God who was telling the story. *But who is the fourth son?* I discovered this fourth son personally while reflecting on Rembrandt's masterpiece 'The Return of the Prodigal'.

I have loved that painting for many years. A copy is displayed in my office and another in my home. One day I was looking at this masterpiece trying to make out the face of the obscure figure in the upper left. The question rose in my mind, "How many observers are there really? Are there others in the darkness or behind the walls?"

In this painting the Elder Brother is depicted as a Pharisee judging the younger brother. The man sitting probably represents the tax-collector who prayed, "Be merciful to me a sinner" (Luke 10:14). There is another figure behind the father watching the drama. She is supposed by some to be a sister, or perhaps the mother. Then there is another up to the far left, outside the circle, looking on. In some reproductions that one is in darkness and cannot be seen. In others he or she is an uninvolved observer.

As I was pondering the possibility that there are others, I suddenly realized I was also observing the drama. I am part of a circle around the father and the prodigal. Am I a Pharisee judging the prodigal and criticizing the father? Or am I in the foreign land trying to find fulfillment outside Father's house? Am I on my way home? Perhaps I am an uninvolved observer like the one in the upper left of Rembrandt's painting, just watching from outside the circle.

So, *the fourth son is the one reading or hearing the story.* We all have a Father in heaven who has given us an inheritance. As we read or hear the story, we are invited to find ourselves in the drama. As a matter of fact, we may be in a different role each time we read or listen. Life moves on, we change, and we need to hear the invitation again in the context of what we have become today. The goal is to spend more and more of our time in Father's embrace.

Three Parables of Lost and Found in Luke 15

As we mentioned, there are two other parables in Luke 15 before we come to the prodigal: the lost sheep, and the lost coin. These three parables have both similarities and differences. For example, all three stories end with rejoicing over what had been found. In the first two the rejoicing is in heaven because a sinner repented. The word repentance is not mentioned in the third parable, but there is rejoicing in the father's heart and in his house.

What can we learn by reading the stories together and comparing them with one another? How can these stories help us in our personal journey? These questions will be the backdrop of our thinking as we seek deeper understand of the meaning of these three parables.

The story of the prodigal begins with the younger son requesting his inheritance. After leaving home he used the money to feel good about himself and look good to others. Like the prodigal, we all have an inheritance from our Father. We have energy and various capacities, abilities, and callings. Father's purpose in giving us these treasures is for us to use them to expand his farm; to advance his kingdom in the earth; to share his love with the world.

By the time we reach adolescence many of us have all learned to use our abilities (our inheritance) to gain a personal advantage over our brothers and sisters and to advance ourselves in the world. We have learned to use our inheritance to feel good about ourselves and look good to others. We do not always share our inner treasures (like compassion and patience) to make life better for others around us.

So, Jesus told these stories to get our attention. Some of us have not yet returned home from the foreign country. We are still trying to feel good about ourselves by spending our inheritance (intelligence, abilities, and energy) on ourselves. Some of us have taken our position in the field as a hired hand trying to earn Father's love, trying to be worthy of his positive attention. Few of us experience Father's embrace regularly.

These meditations are designed to help us locate ourselves and begin a journey deeper into Abba's enduring love. We all cast ourselves in different roles at different times. We are sometimes working in the field, sometimes judging others (like the Elder Brother), and sometimes on our way home. Sometimes we enter the party and enjoy Father's unconditional love for a time.

No matter how close you are to his heart, there is a closer place in him. His bosom is deep and wide. If you are not totally satisfied with your relationship with Abba, simply find yourself in these reflections and follow the path that opens before you. There is a place for you in Father's house today. He is celebrating those who choose to return from the foreign land and from the field.

The Structure of Our Approach

This book is composed of several short meditations collected into sections and chapters. Each section begins with its own introduction. At the end of each short reflection there is a summary statement and a prayer to bring focus to the main point.

In Scripture the name Adam refers to mankind. Literally translated it means man, or mankind. I have occasionally added 'mankind' in parentheses to keep us reminded of that fact.

The word *bosom* refers to the place of intimacy with God available in our daily walk as a Christian on our journey with him into the world today. The bosom is that place *in the Father* from which our true obedience flows. We use the phrase '*Father's embrace* to speak of those moments when we are consciously aware of his presence and his love for us.

Open your heart as you open the book. Drink deeply of Father's love.

Part One

The Shepherd and the Woman

Each of the three parables in Luke 15 has something different to add to the question underlying the situation. For that reason, we can use them to interpret one another.

In this section we consider the first two parables—the lost sheep and the lost coin. These parables help us uncover the overarching concept of returning to our rightful place in the community of our Father's house, entering the joy that is waiting for us there.

The sheep and coin stories both mention repentance as the source of rejoicing in heaven over that which has been found. We will be raising the question of the meaning of repentance in these stories. I was greatly surprised when I began to see that repentance in these passages does not mean what we generally think it means.

The real issue in both stories is the commitment of the shepherd and the woman. The lost condition of the sheep and the coin is only incidental to the real point of these parables. As I pursued more understanding, I saw that neither the shepherd nor the woman assigned blame for being lost. Our Father's love is indeed unconditional. He does not play the blame game.

In this section we have the prodigal story in the back of our minds as we seek insights from the parables of the lost sheep and the lost coin.

Reflection One

The Community Circle

"Now the tax collectors and sinners were all drawing near to hear him. And the Pharisees and the scribes grumbled, saying. This man receives sinners and eats with them." (Luke 15:1-2)

When Jesus spoke, he always addressed a particular audience. He never spoke general platitudes. Many of his statements applied to a group much larger than those present at the time. In that sense his words are also addressed to us in our day. But we can miss the point he is making if we disregard the specific person or group he was speaking to at that time.

There were two basic audiences for these three parables. On one hand there were the scribes and Pharisees; on the other hand, there were the tax collectors and sinners. One group was the insiders of the community circle; the other was the outsiders. You might say the 'haves' and the 'have-nots' of the Jewish religious world of that day.

It is a matter of one's point of view, however, which group was which. From the perspective of the scribes and Pharisees, the tax collectors and sinners were the outsiders. Pharisees considered themselves the standard by which others were judged. If they approved of an action, God would obviously agree with them. If they disapproved, they thought they had a right and a responsibility to judge and sentence the offender.

These leaders were reluctant to associate too closely with Jesus until they saw some evidence that he believed and acted according to their standards. They were not totally closed to him at that time, but neither were they ready to open their circle and let him in. He had not yet proven himself worthy. They did not include him in their circle.

The tax collectors and sinners were different. They did not consider themselves to be the standard. They looked beyond themselves for the model of how they should live. Most were painfully aware that they were not living up to the time-honored requirements of the Law of Moses. Many even compared themselves to the scribes and Pharisees and came up short in their own eyes, condemning themselves for their inability to live up to traditional expectations.

The sinners usually avoided close contact with the Pharisees because they felt their unworthiness when in the presence of such piety. But they were all drawing near to Jesus. Jesus received them and ate with them. The sinners felt comfortable in Jesus' presence because he received them as they were. He saw them from his Father's perspective and did not demand any change before he joined them in their circle. And they accepted him.

From Jesus' viewpoint then, the sinners were the insiders and the Pharisees were the outsiders. The sinners were inside Jesus' circle because they felt at home there, like they were in Abba's house. The Pharisees were outsiders because they chose to keep him out of their circle. They were waiting for Jesus to bow to their imagined superiority and prove himself worthy of their acceptance.

There is a third audience. It is you and me. When Jesus addressed these two groups, he was also addressing all those in every generation who fit into either group. Some of us sinners have seen the Father running to meet us. We have drawn near and felt his acceptance and his embrace.

Some of us have drawn near to Father through Jesus, but we joined the Pharisees working in the field because we still think we are unworthy to enter the house as we are. Sometimes we have even joined the Pharisees in our judgment of others who are enjoying his presence without earning it.

We must learn to see ourselves and others from Father's perspective rather than our own. We can build healthy, intimate relationships only by accepting people as they are.

Prayer

Father open our eyes to see your perspective daily. Help us remain open within your circle. You opened your circle for us. Help us open our circle to others.

13

Reflection Two

Comparing Matthew and Luke

"What man of you, having a hundred sheep, if he has lost one of them, does not leave the ninety-nine in the open country, and go after the one that is lost, until he finds it." (Lk. 15:4)

In Luke's Gospel, Jesus was telling this parable to the scribes and Pharisees who had judged him for receiving sinners, for caring about those outside their circle. The fact that he was addressing these self-appointed judges affects the form and meaning of the text. Jesus' response to the self-righteousness of the religious leaders was a call to self-examination.

One of the best ways to discover the meaning of a text in the Gospels is to compare similar statements, events, or stories in the other Gospels. This is especially true when the immediate context of the story is different in another Gospel. That is the case with the parable of the shepherd and the lost sheep. Jesus probably told many parables about shepherds, each with a slightly different perspective. We find one of those other parables in Matthew.

Matthew recorded a parable about a lost sheep that is different from Luke's in several respects (Matt. 18:10-14). *First,* concerning the audience, Matthew's parable was addressed to disciples in the context of their need to humble themselves as a child (Matt. 18:1-4). It is also related to the statement, *"See to it that you do not despise one of these little ones."* The point of Matthew's parable is that it is not the Father's will that any of these little ones should perish.

In Luke, Jesus addressed his parable to the scribes and Pharisees who had judged him for associating with sinners. It was an attempt to call them out of their self-centered religious pride and exclusivism.

Second, concerning the sheep, in Matthew the other sheep had *"never gone astray" (Matt. 18:13).* Apparently the other ninety-nine in Matthew were those who had humbled themselves as a little child. Those who become like children are the ones who enter the kingdom of heaven.

In Luke, the others *"need no repentance"* (Lk. 15:7). Commentaries generally agree that Jesus was using sarcasm when he spoke of needing no repentance. The implication is that the Pharisees did not recognize or acknowledge their need to change their perspective. So, Luke's parable is designed to call attention to the danger of self-righteousness.

Third, concerning those left behind, in Matthew the other ninety-nine sheep were left on the mountain while the shepherd sought the lost. In biblical imagery mountains often represent being close to God. There may even be a hint of being on top of a holy mountain with Moses, Elisha, and Jesus. It is not a mere coincidence that this parable follows the Transfiguration in Matthew (Matt. 17:1-8). Those who become as children enter the kingdom. They are on the mountain in the presence of the Father with others who have become like children.

In Luke, the other sheep were left in the open country. Open country refers to a deserted, lonely region where sheep are unprotected. They were not on the mountain; they were wandering all around Father's presence (Mount Sinai) but never experiencing intimacy with him. Those who have a righteousness based on keeping the Law are outside the sphere where grace operates (Gal. 5:4). That is a desert place, a wilderness.

From Matthew we learn that humility is necessary to enter the kingdom of heaven. The kingdom is distinct from heaven, by the way. Heaven is 'up there' while the kingdom (rule) of heaven has been 'coming down' out of heaven into the world ever since Jesus visited the sons of Adam. When we add humility to the mix in Luke, we see that humility is related to repentance.

Since the Pharisees were not exhibiting humility, it follows that they were not among those who enter the kingdom as a child. They were not on the mountain. They were in the wilderness wasteland. Pride is always a dead give-away that one has not yet received God's grace. God gives grace to the humble (Js. 4:6).

Humble yourself as a little child so you can be with Father on the mountain.

Prayer

Father keep us mindful of the danger of self-righteousness. Help us acknowledge our need for you to seek us out and find us when we wander.

Reflection Three

Covering and Being Covered

"What man of you, having a hundred sheep, if he has lost one of them, does not leave the ninety-nine in the open country, and go after the one that is lost, until he finds it." (Lk. 15:4)

Most people refer to this passage as the parable of the lost sheep. That is not wrong, but it could hide the real point of the story. When we focus on the sheep rather than the shepherd, we often miss the goodness of the shepherd. When we look at the context more carefully, we see clearly that the real point is the Good Shepherd, not the lost sheep.

Jewish tradition thought of the religious leaders as shepherds of the people. The Christian Church adopted the same practice. The word pastor refers to a shepherd who feeds sheep in the pasture. There are bad pastors who do not care for the sheep, who only use the sheep to make themselves look good, and there are good pastors who nurture the flock. In this parable Jesus is drawing attention to himself as the Good Shepherd who cares for lost sheep, for tax collectors and sinners.

The bad pastors cover their sins lest they appear weak. Those who cover their own sin under religious robes are in a dark and dangerous place. They are in the desert of denial. Our Father's protection is available to those who walk in the light of truth, specifically the truth that they need the Good Shepherd's help. Forgiveness is available to those who confess (uncover) their sin (I Jn. 1:9), not to those who think they need no forgiveness.

Denial is a form of darkness where the truth is covered. Whatever is covered is not exposed to light. When we cover ourselves, we are walking in the darkness of denial. That leaves us vulnerable in the desert. This brand of darkness attracts dark spirits of depression and despair. Pride keeps us from allowing ourselves to be exposed to the light that brings freedom.

When we refuse to acknowledge our sin to ourselves or to others, we are walking away from the light (Jn. 3:20). In our denial we focus on other people and their weaknesses as though their problem excuses any guilt on our part. This darkness also excludes any possibility of intimacy. As long as we focus on others, we are not looking at ourselves.

Why would God leave anyone in the wilderness unprotected? I thought God sent Jesus to save the lost. This question also brings up the issue of the nature of God's sovereignty. Does God's sovereignty mean he is ultimately responsible for everything that happens? No! "Whatever happens is the will of Allah" is an Islamic Statement, not a Christian statement.

The answer is as simple as it is profound. God's sovereignty is the sovereignty of his love, which is more than (but it is not other than) the sovereignty of his will. God's will is to love the world and to have his love rule the earth. Love invites and welcomes, but it does not coerce. Love "does not insist on its own way" (I Cor. 13:4). *Love wants a relationship in freedom.* Control demands conformity and blocks intimacy.

That is why love covers the sins of others (I Pet. 4:8). Love desires intimacy more than right actions. Abba, the only true lover, knows that his love will change you as you receive it. As we uncover ourselves before Abba, something changes deep inside as the light of his love lands in our heart. Those who choose to cover their own sin and spurn that love remain in the open country unprotected like the sheep in the parable.

There can be no intimacy unless both parties are open. If I insist that others be right in every respect before my love is available, it does not matter how much the other desires a relationship, it will never happen until my love covers their shortcomings. God has already covered my sin. He has called me to do the same for others. He wants me to reflect his glory in that way.

It is up to us to respond to his invitation and his welcome. Our Father offers salvation to all, but all do not receive it. Since love does not insist on its own way, we are free to reject the offer. This idea of responding to love does not imply salvation by works, but salvation does require a response of openness on our part, a willingness to receive his covering. You cannot pour water into a closed jar and you cannot pour love into a closed heart.

We must learn to desire intimate relationships more than having things our own way. Intimacy is far more rewarding than being right and proving others wrong.

Prayer

"*Abba, thank you for your invitation. Help us deal with our self-centeredness so we can accept your invitation and experience your loving welcome and share it with others.*"

Reflection Four

Welcoming and Shunning

"And when he has found it, he lays it on his shoulders, rejoicing. And when he comes home, he calls together his friends and his neighbors, saying to them, "Rejoice with me, for I have found my sheep that was lost." (Lk. 15:5-6)

Rejoicing, he put the sheep on his shoulders and carried it home. He did not merely carry the burden of guilt and shame the sheep may have had over being lost, he joyfully carried the sheep. Neither did he reprimand the sheep for getting lost. On the contrary, he threw a party and rejoiced with his friends. The other sheep were still in the wilderness; but the one that had been lost was at home with the shepherd.

The Pharisees who thought they were at home with God were actually in the desert. Those who live in denial, thinking they have no need of repentance, will be left on their own in the wilderness unprotected and vulnerable. But the one who knows he is lost will allow himself to be carried home to Father's embrace.

Home is a place of mutual acceptance and belonging. Wilderness is a place of separation and alienation, a place away from the homeland. The self-righteous Pharisees had their own place, but it was outside Father's family circle. Like the elder brother in the prodigal story, they were in the field working. In their imagination they were the only ones in God's circle, but they were in fact the outsiders.

As long as we try to bring ourselves into fellowship with the Father by obeying rules and regulations, we are out in the wilderness. As long as we gather with others who insist on always being right, we are in the desert community. When we insist that others believe and do everything according to our perception of what is right, we are trying to force them to stay with us in our wasteland of religious pride.

Pharisees kept the wilderness community together by the threat of exclusion. If anyone failed to measure up, they were expelled from the Synagogue. Shunning, and the fear of being shunned, is used in many religious communities to ensure the loyalty of those who are a part. It is conceivable that the lost sheep was lost because the leaders of the wilderness community cast it out of the fold (synagogue).

These religious leaders had a way of covering themselves with attractive robes to hide the fact that they were not as good as they wanted to appear. They only looked good because they were working hard in the religious field, but they were not in fellowship with Abba. They even persecuted any who found rest in Father's love without working for it.

The Good Shepherd keeps his community together by welcoming them just they are. He knows his love has the power to change people. The Law can never change the heart, and life activity comes forth from the heart (Prov. 4:23). Paul saw the dark side of this dilemma when he said, "the power of sin is in the Law" (I Cor. 15:56). When people submit to the Law rather than receiving Abba's unconditional love, sin is empowered in their lives.

Those false shepherds later killed the Good Shepherd because he associated with those who were outside their exclusive circle. But those who received the Good Shepherd's help, allowing themselves to be taken upon his shoulders, found themselves safe in the Father's house with a party arranged in their honor.

The false shepherds and their flocks remained in the wilderness judging those who were rescued without working for it. Those they shunned were carried home to Papa God. Those tax collectors and sinners rejected by the Pharisees were welcome in Father's house.

It is only as we recognize and acknowledge our weakness that we receive his strength. As we honestly face our lost condition, he finds us and takes home.

Prayer

"Thank you, Father. You seek us out and find us when we are lost. Help us see our condition and acknowledge our need in our wilderness so you can take us home."

Reflection Five

Joy in Heaven

"Just so, I tell you, there will be more joy in heaven over one sinner who repents than over ninety-nine righteous persons who need no repentance." (Lk. 15:7)

There is joy in heaven when a sinner repents. But we have difficulty locating repentance in the parable itself. We have trouble because we think repentance is something we do, an act we perform. What did the sheep do in this parable that might be called repentance? "He came back home," you say. No, Jesus *carried* the sheep back home. The return home was not a work of the sheep. It was a work of the shepherd.

The parable as it appears in this text does not contain anything the sheep did. "He wandered from the fold," some say. But the parable as it stands does not say the sheep strayed from the fold. The sheep may have wandered away, but that is not the point of this parable.

The shepherd lost the sheep. "If he [the shepherd] lost one," the parable says. *The emphasis of this parable is on the shepherd's loss, not the sheep's condition.* This is a parable of the Good Shepherd. The shepherd took full responsibility for the sheep's lost condition and assigned no blame to the sheep. *His steadfast love endures forever.*

So, the real point is not that the sheep 'got lost,' at least not as the parable reads. The parable takes no notice of any act of the sheep in becoming separated, nor does it report any act of the sheep in returning. It is all about the commitment of the Good Shepherd to his sheep.

In Luke 5:32 Jesus said, "I have not come to call the righteous but sinners to repentance." Saul of Tarsus considered himself righteous according to the law, but when the Good Shepherd appeared to him, he knew he was chief of sinners. What did Saul do to prompt Jesus to appear to him and send him into the world as an apostle? Absolutely nothing. Saul was chosen from his mother's womb. He did not know it, but belonged long before Jesus came to him.

"But Saul changed," you say. Yes, he did change, but it was the presence of Jesus on the Damascus Road that changed him. The change was an act of God, not an act of Saul. Saul just allowed himself to be carried on the Shepherd's shoulders in his journey into the world to find more lost sheep.

As long as we think of ourselves as having a righteousness based on anything we do, we have not yet heard the call of Jesus. He has called all men to repentance, but all men do not hear the call. Many think they are okay and need no help from the Shepherd.

True righteousness is a grace-gift from Abba Father. It does affect our behavior, but our behavior is not responsible for the change. The Shepherd does the work.

It is as though Jesus came to the Pharisees and said, "I came to call sinners into the fellowship of the Father." And the Pharisees responded, "We already have God's favor, but we know where you can find those sinners. They are on the other side of town or in the country, far away from this religious center. We do not allow any sinners in our group. If you associate with them, we will reject you as well." So, Jesus went away from the religious center to find the sinners who were outcasts, who were lost and knew they needed finding. He was a fellow outcast.

It is a sad fact that some church families exclude 'sinners' from their fellowship. They may have a doctrine of grace, but they do not practice it. They seem to think that their holy place would be defiled if 'those people' came in. Their rule is that you must believe all the right things and do all the right things before you can belong in their circle.

The holy One of Israel is comfortable with allowing sinners in his presence. He knows his presence will change them. When the sinner experiences change, he or she will believe.

Prayer

Father we acknowledge that other sinners are as welcome in your bosom as we are. Help us remove the judge's robe, put down our gavel, and receive other sinners.

Reflection Six

Seeing Differently

"Just so, I tell you, there will be more joy in heaven over one sinner who repents than over ninety-nine righteous persons who need no repentance." (Lk 15:7)

What then is repentance? The New Testament word for repentance means to see things differently, to have a change of perspective. The sheep was probably too preoccupied to notice she was lost. When the shepherd found her, she suddenly saw herself in anew light. She realized two things at once, that she was lost and that her shepherd had found her. She did not resist the shepherd; she allowed herself to be carried home to a party she did not deserve.

When revelation breaks through, repentance happens. A change of direction is not the essence of repentance, but it is a significant result. Repentance is the result of being found and suddenly seeing yourself differently. If there is not at least a small change, we might question whether we have actually repented. Perhaps we have only been sorry over our condition without recognizing the Shepherd or perhaps we have only been sorry that we were caught.

It is possible to change directions without realizing the truth, but it is a hassle to maintain that new direction when we change without true repentance. That is because the change was not based on a revelation of Father's love. "You will know the truth, and the truth will make you free," Jesus said (Jn. 8:31). Truth received in the heart changes us; our will power in deciding to turn does not, at least not permanently.

It is only when we wake up that we realize we were dreaming. We do not even realize we are sleeping until we begin to come to consciousness again. It is like that when we are lost. I love hiking in the mountains. I once wandered around on a mountain for a long time thinking I knew where I was. But suddenly I saw something that told me I was not where I thought I was. I repented—I saw things differently—but I was not home yet. I had to change my direction, and I was motivated to do so.

So, repentance is simply allowing ourselves to be exposed as those who need to be found and brought back home. That is what happened to Saul of Tarsus. When our eyes are opened to see Abba's goodness, we automatically rejoice at being found and trust the Shepherd to carry us to the party.

But the Pharisees refused to see the truth about their condition. Jesus found them but they would not acknowledge they were lost. They pulled their righteous robes tightly around themselves and accused Jesus of having a demon (Jn. 8:48). After all, he did not accept them as stalwart examples of righteousness. Their self-righteousness kept them from responding to his call for sinners to come to him and receive forgiveness. As a result, repentance did not happen in them; they did not see things differently.

The opposite of repentance is insisting that you already know the truth and have no need to listen to anything that contradicts what you already believe. Those who think they know everything cannot hear the truth because they are not listening. In other words, the opposite of repentance is pride. God resists the proud and gives grace to the humble.

The proud prefer to focus on the changes they have made in their own strength. That way they can feel good about themselves and look good to others who have not been able to change as much as they have. Their robes really do make them look good, but their robes do not glorify God. Instead they glorify human effort. As long the Pharisees focus on their own goodness, they are blind to the truth of Father's unconditional love.

The proud are closed to anything that might expose the fact that they are not as right as they think they are. The humble are always ready to receive more understanding, even if it requires a change in their way of seeing and doing things. The proud want to force everyone else to change and conform to their ideal. The humble want to experience change personally.

Repentance is seeing things differently and allowing yourself to be brought to a party you do not deserve.

Prayer

"Lord thank you that you do not require us to find our own way back home. Keep us reminded that we continually need your help and your guidance."

Reflection Seven

The Woman and the Coin

"Or what woman, having ten silver coins, if she loses one coin, does not light a lamp and sweep the house and seek diligently until she finds it? And when she has found it, she calls together her friends and neighbors, saying, 'Rejoice with me, for I have found the coin that I had lost.' Just so, I tell you, there is joy before the angels of God over one sinner who repents." (Luke 75:8-10)

This next parable is about a woman who lost a coin. It seems to me that Jesus told this parable just in case we missed the point of the previous parable. A coin obviously can do nothing to get lost or to return to its proper place. So, this parable is not so much about the coin but about the commitment of the woman to find it.

The coin was a *drachma*, a silver coin worth only a few dollars at most. If the coin were the issue she could easily go to work and replace it. Some have suggested the coin was part of much larger engagement gift from the bridegroom or his father. That would place the value of the coin in the context of intimacy and relationship. To lose this coin could be interpreted as dishonoring the bridegroom.

The ten coins may have been worked into a band to wear across the forehead to identify the bride as belonging to the groom. When others saw the engagement band, they would know she is not available. So, the loss of the coin represents a loss in the integrity of the bride's relationship to the groom. The coin's true value is far beyond its monetary value.

The gifts from Father God and his son also identify us as belonging. When we received him and believed in his name we were sealed with the promised Holy Spirit (Eph. 1:13-14). This would also include the gifts of the Spirit—love, joy, peace, etc. When we fail to publicly display the gifts, we hide the fact that we belong to him. This is like losing part of the engagement pledge.

The woman was diligent to seek until she found what she had lost. She was aware of its true value as a pledge and a sign of belonging. She did not merely want a coin *like* the one she lost. She wanted *that* coin because it was a sign of the intimate bond between her and her betrothed. She would not quit seeking until she found the treasure.

Many within the Bride of Christ lose coins and do not even notice they are missing. They simply go on with life as though their relationship with the Bridegroom is okay. After all, they go to church every Sunday and tithe regularly (some of them). They never look in the mirror of the Word to see themselves, or if they do, they conveniently forget what they saw (Js. 1:24).

Some try to work to earn a coin to replace what was lost. But the relationship will never heal by the Bride's working and earning more coins. Those who work in the religious field (like the Elder Brother) may earn many coins *like* the gift from the Father and the Son, but they are counterfeit. Unfortunately, most people will never notice the difference.

The fieldworkers impress one another with their earnings and think their accomplishments give them a place of importance. They even rank themselves according to who has earned more coins than others. The one with the most coins thinks he has a right to exclude others with fewer coins. There is no possibility of intimacy in this kind of community.

They seldom stop to notice they are not in the house enjoying intimacy with the Bridegroom. In fact, they are usually jealous of those enjoying the house-party who have not earned any coins. They think, "Those sinners have to prove themselves worthy before they deserve the robe of righteousness the Father gave them for the party." It seems so unfair to those who have earned so many coins.

Working to make up for our loss of intimacy seems to be part of our inheritance from Adam. It is so natural that we have trouble accepting grace as a gift.

Prayer

Father, we acknowledge our tendency to try to earn your gifts. Help us to see your grace for what it is—a free gift and a pledge of covenant.

Reflection Eight

Lighting a Lamp

"Or what woman, having ten silver coins, if she loses one coin, does not light a lamp and sweep the house and seek diligently until she finds it? And when she has found it, she calls together her friends and neighbors, saying, 'Rejoice with me, for I have found the coin that I had lost.' Just so, I tell you, there is joy before the angels of God over one sinner who repents." (Luke 15:8-10)

It is difficult to find something that is covered in darkness. Light is required. Father sent his Son into the dark world as light. Jesus said, "I am the light of the world." His mission was to find what his Father had lost.

But this is a woman lighting a lamp. This is not a male figure as the shepherd is. What does this suggest?

Jesus also said, *"You are the light of the world... let your light shine before others, so that they may see your good works and give glory to your Father who is in Heaven." (Matt. 5:14-16)*

When the Bride wears the coins, she lets the light of Father's glory shine into the world. That is why it is so important that we find the coin if we have lost it. We are unable to reflect the glory of our Bridegroom by mere good deeds. Father's light only shines from the genuine coins, from the work of the Holy Spirit in our lives. If anyone ever comes to Father's house through something we have said or done, it will be the light of Father's glory that drew them.

So, Abba uses light reflecting from our coins to find what he lost. But the light in this parable is from a lamp, not from the coins. She was seeking something she lost, not what the father lost. She had lost the ability to reflect the fullness of the glory of her bridegroom and his father. One coin was missing, and with the missing part, the wholeness of the gift and its ability to bear witness to God's glory was compromised.

How do we lose the coin? It is easy to lose things when the house (our life) is cluttered. The other things in the house keep demanding our attention. Important things are often lost in the shuttle. We can be so concerned with the external appearance of the 'house' that we fail to exhibit the coins that signal we belong to another. When we neglect them and do not keep them on display, they get lost.

When this happens (as it often does with all of us), our commitment to the gift is exposed—whether strong or weak. If we notice its absence and do not try to find it, we parade the fact that it does not mean much to us. Or if we try for a short time and give up, we demonstrate that other things are more important to us"

"Your word is a lamp to my feet and a light to my path" (Ps. 119:105). The coin is intimately related to our walk on the path of life, to how we present ourselves to others. It is the Word of the

Lord that expels the darkness that hides the coin we have lost. When a coin is missing, we need to receive his Word and allow it to expose what is hidden in darkness under the clutter of our life. The Word shows which gift is missing, whether love, joy, or peace, etc. And from the lighted Lamp and the Spirit we receive it back again.

The woman searched diligently for the coin. To find it, she used the lighted lamp (Scripture seen through the eyes of the Spirit) to see beyond the clutter in her house. When she found the coin, she invited her friends to rejoice with her—just like the Good Shepherd who found his sleep. This time, however, it is the Bride rejoicing because she had found the Bridegroom's gift and displayed it again.

This parable also ends with the issue of repentance. What did the coin do? Absolutely nothing. But the woman did work diligently to remove all clutter to bring the coin into the light. The coin simply allowed itself to be present while the woman celebrated with her friends.

Diligence in seeking to find what we lost is evidence of a strong commitment to displaying the gift. We always make a great effort to get what we really want. And rejoicing before the angels always follows finding.

Prayer

Lord, help us to take the gift seriously, alert us to what is missing in our lives and bring us back to our connection with the Bridegroom with the coins on exhibit.

41

Part Two

Parting Company

Now we are ready to look at the story of the lost son. In this chapter we consider the various issues involved in the son's leaving his father's house. The end of the parable shows the father to be a good father and the house to be a place of joy and rejoicing. That raises a question: Why did this younger son want to leave?

In this parable we will find that the story is really about the goodness of the father. The word prodigal refers to one who gives or spends lavishly and recklessly. With that definition in mind we could call this the parable of the *Prodigal Father*. He was lavish and reckless in giving the inheritance to a son who was not yet mature enough to use it wisely.

He was also lavish and reckless when he received the son back into fellowship without demanding penance. So, this is the story of a good father who lost a son. The father's loss is more central to the story than the son's condition even though we must never ignore the son's condition.

The point of this parable is that Abba Father is a good Father who lost a son (humanity). He is lavish in pouring blessings on the just and the unjust (Matt. 5:45). He is a Prodigal Father. Our Father loves with unconditional, enduring love. But that love can be rejected and despised. When that happens, Father's arms are forever waiting with an embrace and a party honoring the returning son. He is the Waiting Father.

Reflection Nine

Inheritance and Property

"There was a man who had two sons. And the younger of them said to his father, 'Father, give me the share of property that is coming to me.' And he divided his property between them." (Luke. 15:11-12)

The younger son did not ask for his inheritance; he asked for property. An inheritance is what a father passes on to his sons and daughters. It includes the possessions, but it is not limited to the articles and assets the father owns. There are other things a father can bequeath to his children, like wisdom, honor, and a basic perspective of life and relationships. These qualities have more value than stuff, but young boys do not know that.

During childhood and adolescence, inheritance is generally equated with monetary value. At that age we do not really appreciate the part of the inheritance that has to do with character development. Material goods have substance. We think of what money can buy rather than what wisdom can bring into our lives. Some, perhaps most, never outgrow this perspective.

The more valuable part of the inheritance, the things of the heart, do not simply pass from good fathers to sons as a matter of course. They are developed in the process of relating to the father. They come only as the sons and daughters spend intimate time with their father. If there is no relationship, there will be a limit to the portion of inheritance they can receive.

This son's focus was on the possessions rather than the inheritance. He failed to discover the heart of his father. He lost track of who he was as a son of a good father. He began to think of all the things he could have and do if he could sell some of the stuff his Father had. And he certainly did not want his father tagging along while he did those things. Who would want God to tag along while we waste our inheritance?

In adolescence (and subsequent years if we do not mature) we are more interested in the stuff our dad has than in who he is. Few kids of that age see value in having a relationship with him. Knowing him and being known by him usually does not hold their attention. They are generally more interested in feeling good about themselves and looking good to their peers. That is why there are so many family fights when the inheritance (stuff) is being divided

We do the same thing in our relationship with our heavenly Father. We focus on what he can do for us, how he can rescue us out of our problems and provide what we need for a good life. He certainly wants to provide, but this mind-set causes us to miss the character qualities our Father desires to impart to us. We miss out on the real inheritance of the saints—conformity to the image of the firstborn Son.

Or we focus on the things he requires of us. We want to earn his approval by working in the religious field. We want to do more than others so we will look good to our fellow workers and feel good about ourselves. We seldom see that we already look good in our Father's eyes. We seldom see because we seldom look in his eyes to see our reflection. We should already feel good about ourselves because of who we are as his sons and daughters.

Our focus on material goods and provisions indicates that we do not see value in spending time with Abba Father to receive impartation and direction for our lives. This positions us outside Father's house. We are still sons and daughters, but we act as though we have no Father in heaven. We think and act like spiritual orphans. Whether in the field or in the foreign land, we are fatherless and homeless in our hearts.

The real inheritance is Father's love. It remains ours even when we waste the property. He still wants to impart his heart of love to us so we can pass it on.

Prayer

Father help us focus on what you desire to give us rather on what we think would be good for us. We want to have your heart of love for others.

Reflection Ten

Seeing and Reflecting

"There was a man who had two sons. And the younger of them said to his father, 'Father, give me the share of property that is coming to me.' And he divided his property between them." (Luke. 15:11-12)

The younger brother was with his father in the house before he left for the foreign country. But he never really saw his father, he only saw the property. We tend to become conformed to the image of what we behold with reverence. He was a son of his father, with his father's DNA, but he did not reflect his father's character because he did not see his father accurately. He did not see because he only looked at the property.

We can only know what manner of man or woman we really are by seeing ourselves reflected in Abba's eyes. If we never look, we will never see ourselves mirrored there. We can become conformed to his image only if we see him as he is. We are loved and often we do not know it because we do not gaze into his approving eyes. If we knew him intimately, we would not try to fill the father-void with other things or activities.

This separation from the Father and from our true selves sets us up to misuse the property he makes available to us. When Adam (humanity), separated himself from the Father by eating the forbidden fruit, God allowed him to maintain access to all the property that was coming to him—all except the Tree of Life which is only available for those who are intimate with Father. The fruit of that tree produces the character of God in those who eat.

Adam was still in the world. All things were still available to him. But he could not enjoy all the good things because he did not relate to Father God. He believed the enemy's lie and began to think of God as a hard taskmaster. We, like Adam, will never fully enjoy the property until we begin to abide in the embrace of Abba Father and partake of the Tree of Life.

As we said earlier, we become orphans in our thinking when we try to live apart from our Father. Orphans have no inheritance. Inheritance is only available to sons and daughters. In this condition we are not only separated from the Father, we are also separated from our true selves. We are not in touch with who we really are as sons and daughters because we are not in touch with our Father.

Orphans must make it on their own. They must earn, beg for, or steal everything they get. They have no expectation that anyone will give them anything without some effort on their part. "*If it's going to be, it's up to me*" is the theme of their lives. Despite all their efforts, they never have enough, they are never content. They always want more because their earnings, their achievements, and their status are never enough to fill the father-void.

If we find ourselves trying to make it on our own, it might indicate orphan thinking. Begging God for something he has already given also comes from the orphan spirit. We beg because we cannot conceive of Abba giving us something simply because he loves us. We try to move him to have pity on us. Perhaps we beg because we feel like an outcast with no right to the things Abba has already made available to us.

The orphan heart is exposed in many other ways as well. But how do we get rid of this way of thinking? Jack Frost often said, "You cannot cast out an orphan spirit. You can only introduce people to the Father who loves them." When they see him differently, they will see themselves differently and change.

We must shift our focus from the property to our glorious inheritance. Being conformed to the image of the firstborn Son and having his Father as our Father is more satisfying than having stuff available.

Prayer

Lord, introduce yourself to us again today. Bring us back to sonship. Let us walk with you and receive the inheritance. Impart your heart of love to us.

Reflection Eleven

Rights and Responsibilities

"And the younger of them said to his father, "Father, give me the share of property that is coming to me.' And he divided his property between them." (Lk. 15:12)

The property was coming to him. The younger son asked for what already belonged to him. The father would have given him authority to manage it as soon as he was mature enough to handle it responsibly. The father was waiting for him to demonstrate the wisdom necessary to care for the assets and keep the farm productive. This son was not willing to wait for wisdom to develop. That is foolish.

It was Father God's intention to give the earth to Adam's race from the beginning. Even today, *the meek will inherit the earth* (Matt. 5:5). Our Father has already given his sons and daughters full authority in the earth. As soon as they exhibit the quality of meekness, they will be able to exercise that authority to expand the 'farm' into all the world. Adam (humanity) failed to value intimacy with God and for that reason failed to develop meekness and receive the full inheritance.

The full inheritance was not to come to Adam until he had developed the image of God that was already in him in seed form. If he had received daily from the Tree of Life, he would have been able to exercise loving authority over creation. Instead, he had the property with little wisdom or ability to manage it properly. Adam is still devouring his portion of the property which he should be developing.

The image of God is Love; and love is meek. Love does not take, it gives. Love does not insist on its own way (I Cor.13). Our Father wants us to rule and reign with him in the earth, but his reign is a reign of love. So, our Father is waiting for us to receive the more valuable portion of the inheritance—the image of his love in the firstborn Son. We will not reign with him until we develop his character and learn to reign in love.

There have been many Bible teachers calling the Church to "possess your possessions." That is very biblical, but it is usually presented with the attitude of the prodigal son. "Take what's rightfully yours. God promised it to you." That sounds much like the younger brother on his way to the foreign country. Many may have embraced this message because it struck a chord in their orphan heart.

God has promised, but he may be withholding what he promised because he knows we would misuse it. He knows how easily we believe the lies of the enemy. We are not ready to possess our possessions until we learn to refuse and reject the lies of the enemy. Although Father often withholds, he sometimes gives us what we demand and allows us to waste it.

This orphan spirit is especially prevalent in the American Church. America has developed an attitude of entitlement. Our "Bill of Rights" is destroying us. We need a "Bill of Responsibilities." The spirit of entitlement causes us to sue one another for large sums. We want to be rich at the expense of others. We want to get 'what's coming to us' even if it costs others their life sustenance. That attitude does not reflect Father's love.

When we press to have our inheritance before we are mature enough to rule in love, we waste the property. We also waste ourselves and damage others in the process. That is what the prodigal did. Trying to gain a feeling of being important, we spend the inheritance on things that do not satisfy. Father's property is transferred into the hands of the enemy, we are wasted, lost to our birthright, and the father-void remains.

We must desire maturity more than we desire the property. That means we must desire a relationship with the Father that will bring us to maturity.

Prayer

Father help us put off the spirit of entitlement and put on the spirit of meekness. Help us to become more like your firstborn Son. We want to bear his image of love.

Reflection Twelve

Unconditional Love

"And the younger of them said to his father, 'Father, give me the share of property that is coming to me.' And he divided his property between them." (Lk. 15:12)

The father divided his property between the two brothers. The text gives no indication of the attitude of the father, but the apparent peace and confidence with which the father divided his possessions is amazing. No doubt he was disappointed and wounded by the younger son's disregard for the relationship between them. Yet he bountifully bestowed the blessing on his son. That was indeed an act of prodigal extravagance. Our Father sends rain on the just and the unjust.

The son now has the property without the wisdom to manage it. Why would a father do that? Perhaps because he thinks the son will learn the hard way. But that is taking a great risk. What if the son does not learn? Most earthly fathers are not willing to take that risk. Our heavenly Father took that risk when he gave his Son over to the Jews and the Romans. Abba believed his love would win the day his Son by relying on his Father.

I suggest that the prodigal's father trusted the power of his love to bring his son back when his son hit bottom. His love for his son did not allow him to become angry or bitter. This is certainly true of our heavenly Father. He had a plan. Abba Father sent his firstborn Son, the Son of his love, as an emissary of his love. He knows his love can heal the breach we caused by our rebellion if we will only receive it as the free gift he offers.

Our Father will allow us to go our own way and forsake him. He does not withdraw his love when we reject Him. Love "does not insist on its own way" (I Cor. 13:5). Love is not controlling or manipulating. God is Love. Our Father will release us to do as we please; but he will always be waiting for us to come to ourselves and return to his house. He is the Waiting Father whose love is unconditional. His steadfast love endures forever, even when we refuse it.

True love is freely given. When there are strings attached, it is not true love; it is self-serving. As Bob Mumford often said, that kind of love has a hook in it. True love desires to be loved freely in return. Love wants a relationship in freedom. A love that is demanding and controlling does not really want intimacy, it only wants to have its own way. That is the devil's counterfeit love. That imitation love tries to control and breeds rebellion, independence, and broken relationships.

This helps us with a question that often comes up. "Why does God not keep us from doing things that will hurt us?" God knows that control breeds rebellion. When our parents or other authorities in our lives tried to control us, we locked ourselves up against intimacy and went our own way. Some of us have done that openly in rebellion, others simply by withdrawing inwardly and ceasing to relate. Either way, the family tie is broken.

One reason we have trouble being close to our heavenly Father is that we have closed ourselves off to our earthly fathers. We think God is like our earthly dad, so we shut him out as well. In this closed condition we cannot have true intimacy with anyone, not even God. Abba is not withholding himself from us; we are closed to the love he has for us. His love is for sinners. It is for us. His steadfast love endures forever, but we must be open to receive it.

Closed is closed. If I have a jar with a lid on it, nothing inside can come out and nothing outside can get in. Our heart is like that. When we shut down to a fellowman, we are also shut down to God's love. Jesus said, "*...as you did it to one of the least of these my brothers, you did it to me*" (Matt. 25:40). As a result, when the water of the Spirit is poured out, we may get wet. It feels good for the moment, but we remain empty. Nothing gets in. The father-void remains.

We must walk toward healing the broken relationships with our fellowmen before we can experience the fullness of Father's embrace.

Prayer

Father thank you for loving us despite of our selfishness. Help us to repair our relationships with men and women in our lives so we can receive the fullness of your love.

59

Part Three

Seeking Fulfillment

The younger son thought he could find more of the good life in the foreign land than he had in the presence of his father. Someone said, "Be careful what you seek. You may find it and discover it is not what you thought it would be."

The prodigal began by looking for the wrong things, for diversions that could not be found in his father's house. True intimacy was available there, and the delight of that intimacy far outweighs any earthly pleasure. Human nature was designed by God to seek this satisfaction from Father God. Our Daddy God wants us to find fulfillment in him, not because he is self-centered but because he knows how he created us.

The prodigal could not find what he wanted in father's house, so he began looking in the wrong place and found the counterfeit. Like the fruit of the forbidden tree, the imitation looked good and promised a reward. When the prize brought only temporary fulfillment to the prodigal, he tried to compensate for the continued emptiness by doing the same thing again thinking perhaps he did not do it hard enough or long enough. And again, he found misery and emptiness rather than joy and fulfillment. The father-void remained.

This young brother found many other things—the pleasures of sin that give temporary fulfillment. He probably stumbled on to some other young bucks who liked to have a good time with him. The admiration of others was readily available because he had money. He was using his inherited property trying to feel good about himself and look good to his peers.

He found a false sense of security. As long as his money held out, he was oblivious to the lack that was on its way into his life. His awareness of the coming doom was blocked out by the temporary fun and favor he was experiencing. But what did he really discover? What did he really find? Read on.

Reflection Thirteen

The Empty Land

"Not many days later, the younger son gathered all he had and took a journey into a far country, and there he squandered his property in reckless living." (Lk. 15:13)

This was the ultimate insult to the father. Not only did he ask for the property before the father died, he left home and used it in reckless living. The prodigal transferred his portion of his father's wealth into the hands of those outside the family by his reckless spending. The father must have been wounded deeply by this. The prodigal son was behaving just like Adam who transferred Father's property into the enemy's hands.

We noticed earlier that the father had an inheritance for his sons other than property. The most significant part of our inheritance is Abba's love. Wisdom and knowledge are also available. To receive those, we must spend quality time with our Father. Adam (humanity) tried to gain knowledge by eating from the forbidden tree rather than by spending time with God. The prodigal tried to gain love by spending his inheritance rather than receiving from his father.

The phrase 'foreign country' in the Greek can refer to an empty expanse, even a gaping chasm, far away from home. The root of this word is the source of our *English word chasm*. The concept is like the wilderness in the lost sheep story. The younger son was not aware of the emptiness facing him on the journey he had chosen. He only saw the false promise of a good time. He did not realize he was headed for a deep pit.

The word in the text for 'squander' is sometimes used for the process of winnowing. The grain was thrown up into the air and the wind blew away the chaff and the seed fell to the ground. This son threw his money into the wind and lost everything - everything except the seed of his father's love. But he did not yet know his father's love.

Reckless living is living in a way that depletes resources and defiles the sense of health and wholeness ('reckless' is from *asozo*, the negation of *sozo*, which means salvation, or wholeness). That which promises life produces death. That which promises fulfillment produces emptiness. Living outside Father's house is living in futility, in an empty expanse. The more we try to find fulfillment, the more we lose touch with the Father's love. We also lose touch with our true selves and with all meaningful relationships.

That is what it means to be lost. Being lost has more to do with life in this world than most people think. The issue is not hell after death, it is about hell on earth while you are on your way to death. Returning is about finding life in Father's presence here and now, life on the way to more life.

Father's intention is to bring the kingdom of heaven here. The kingdom of heaven is the rule of love in our hearts and, through us, love reigning in the earth. This kingdom has been coming since Jesus lived among us in his flesh. Life reigns over death since his resurrection. It comes to us and through us as we yield our lives to its influence and give Abba's love to others. Resurrection life here and now is our inheritance.

Ever since Adam (humanity) tried to find life through created things (the forbidden tree), he has been wandering around in a gaping chasm outside the garden trying to find something to make him feel loved, something that makes him feel like he has value as a person. Love and worth are the true inheritance our Father has for us. Jesus came to this far country to win us back to Daddy's enduring love.

Many are still looking for fulfillment in this empty expanse. They are numb to reality. They spend their energy and resources trying to have fun or be comfortable. Only later they realize they were not really having fun, nor were they comfortable. They see that they were only grasping at straws trying to gain what they felt like they lost—their Father's love. They were not aware that Father's love for them endures forever.

The only way to find true health and wholeness is to respond to the Son's call to return to Father's welcoming embrace. As long as we continue to try to find life outside Father's bosom, we will remain in the foreign country. Even some who are 'born again' choose to remain in the foreign country trying to find love and comfort in all the wrong places. Our Father will not allow us to find fulfillment there because it is a place of death.

Let us wake up to the Father's love and choose to find our fulfillment in his bosom. Let us take back the inheritance we have given over to the enemy and make it available for the advancing Kingdom of God.

Prayer

Lord, thank you for your unconditional love. Help us to stop trusting in the things of this world, thinking they can give us what only you can give.

Reflection Fourteen

Consuming and Being Consumed

"Not many days later, the younger son gathered all he had and took a journey into a far country, and there be squandered his property in reckless living." (Lk. 15:13)

The food you eat becomes a part of you. But what you chose to consume greedily will eventually consume you. You will also become a part of what consumes you. We will consume something, and we will be consumed by something. That is the reality of life in this world. You can be self-consumed or consumed by work, or play, or desire. Life is a series of choices as to which consumption you will experience.

This young man chose to consume those things that made him feel good in his loneliness. He partook of emptiness and became empty. The text does not mention any details, but alcohol and women were likely a part of his daily pursuit. As he took those things for himself, he also gave himself to them. Little did he realize he was diminishing as a person even as his finances decreased. *He was giving himself away with his inheritance.*

He was devouring and being devoured by what he used to make himself feel good and look good. If he was anything like modern men, the more he took in, the more he wanted. He was spending and being spent in the process. But he was too focused on medicating his pain to notice the loss. He thought one more drink or one more woman would solve his problem.

There is a different kind of consumption available, a consumption that is rewarding. "Our God is a consuming fire" (Heb. 12:29). When he shows up on the scene, everything unholy is consumed. His presence reduces his enemies to ashes. Those who desire to be integrated into his family circle will find themselves in his bosom with all their ungodliness consumed.

The Song of Songs expresses this insight in this way: "*You have captivated [ravished] my heart, my sister, my bride; you have captivated my heart with one glance of your eyes, with one jewel of your necklace.*" *(Song of Solomon 4:9)*

If we allow our bridegroom to ravish our heart, we will also ravish his heart. When we take him to heart, he has already taken us to heart. This is mutual consumption at its best. Consuming him in love and being consumed by his love is the way life was designed to be. Jesus' goal for our lives is, "*that they may all be one just as you, Father, are in me, and I in you that they also may be in us*" (Jn. 17:21). His love endures forever. Those who abide in his love endure with his love—forever.

The only wise choice is to allow yourself to be consumed by the unconditional love of Abba Father. We noted earlier that the word for reckless living (*asozo*) is a negative form of the word translated salvation, being brought into a state of health and wholeness. Too often we limit the concept of salvation to heaven after we die. It is much more than that. It also includes living a fulfilled life here and now, consumed by and consuming Abba's love.

This choice is not made in your head; it is not an intellectual endeavor. The choice comes from the heart. "Keep your heart with all vigilance, for from it flow the springs of life" (Prov. 4:23). If it were a matter of logic, everyone would obviously choose life in Love. But our hearts are cluttered with other desires that move us to consume and be consumed by other things.

The clutter in our heart needs to be removed before we will be able to effectively choose life in Love. But we are powerless to change ourselves. That clutter must be consumed by the fire of Father's love for us. That consuming fire will fall on all who take the risk of submitting to it. Yes, you will be consumed. You will be consumed and taken into the life of God.

Today is the day of salvation, the day to choose life in Love. Today is the day to consume and be consumed by his love.

Prayer

"Create in me a clean heart, O God, and renew a right spirit within me" (Ps. 51:10). Lord, only you can change us on the inside. Help us yield our heart to your approach.

Reflection Fifteen

Feast and Famine

"And when he had spent everything, a severe famine arose in that country, and he began to be in need." (Lk. 15:14)

"When he had spent everything...." The property back home is still producing abundantly. Real property, land, will never be spent if it is cared for. But when we convert property into ready cash, it blows away with the wind. Cash has no ability to reproduce itself. It will not replenish itself. The boy could have learned this lesson at home if he had focused on his relationship with his father rather than on the property.

"A severe famine arose in that country." Famine does not necessarily bring disaster. Two people living in the same neighborhood may experience the crisis quite differently. For one it may be a place of growth and development. For the other it becomes a place of stagnation and depression.

The younger son was empty and unproductive. There was more missing in his life than food. The external environment began to expose his destitute inner state. He was void of food for

71

his spirit. He was hungry for love-food that only his father could provide. But he had walked away from the source that could meet that need.

"He began to be in need." He became consciously aware of the defect in his way of approaching life. His inner famine had oozed to the surface. He had this defect, this need, before he left his father's house. It was this void that prompted him to leave. At this point in the story he was forced to face his emptiness. This was the beginning of a life of mature sonship for him, but he did not know that yet. It would be through this dark valley that he would become his father's son in his heart.

We seldom realize the value of hard times when they first hit us in the gut. Our first response is usually anger, despair, fear, or depression. The Good Shepherd who leads us to green pastures also leads us through the valley dark as death (Ps. 23). In that valley we become aware of our enemies. It is also a place to trust in his presence and provision. He prepares a feast for us in the in the presence of our enemy, in the land of famine. That feast is not limited to food.

When our focus is on the enemy and the dark valley, we become blind to the presence of the Shepherd who is with us in the valley. We do not even notice the table he prepared for us there. Our perception is limited to the negative elements of the situation. In other words, we begin to be more aware of our need than we are of his provision. We do not see that all our needs have been supplied (Phil. 4:13). We experience a famine of love-food in the gaping chasm of the foreign land and fail to receive Abba's love.

We must learn to shift our focus to the Shepherd who is with us as we go through the valley. The valley is still dark, but we can feast in the presence of the one who loves us. He will never leave us or forsake us. And he is committed to finish his work in us until we are conformed to his image and reflect his glory. That is our inheritance in his house. That is what approaches us as we respond to Father's love in the dark valley.

In Luke's Good Shepherd parable, the shepherd did not return the sheep to the wilderness. He was available to all the sheep in the wilderness as a way out. The other ninety-nine (Pharisees) could have responded to the presence of Father's love, it was also available to them. But they denied their need for that love, they even denied they were in a dark valley.

When we acknowledge we are in the valley and experience its darkness, there we learn to value the presence of the Good Shepherd. His intention, however, is not to leave us in the gaping chasm but to bring us home.

Inheritance comes to sons and daughters who are in fellowship with the Father. Fellowship involves a focus on the one who is with you in green pastures as well as in the valley. He is the one who will carry you home to Father's house.

Prayer

Father, thank you for the opportunities you allow for us to grow closer to you. Help us shift our focus from our circumstances (good or bad) to your presence.

Reflection Sixteen

Freedom and Bondage

"So, he went and hired himself out to one of the citizens of that country who sent him into his fields to feed pigs." (Lk. 15:15)

The path away from Father's house is downhill. *"There is a way that seems right to a man, but its end is the way of death"* (Prov. 14:12). The promise of freedom in the foreign land is deceptive. Freedom defined as the absence of restriction is really bondage. The taskmasters of this freedom will tease you with fun and excitement until you are trapped. In the book of Proverbs, those who go for that bait are called fools.

The son's journey away from his father's embrace began long before he asked for the property. Apparently, the prodigal had felt like a hired hand in his father's business to begin with. As the father was trying to train him in the art of productivity, he felt trapped, like he was in a prison. Perhaps he even felt abused.

When you are focused on the task, it is easy to feel used or abused. That feeling was itself the original deception for the prodigal. He did not believe his father had his best interest in mind. He thought his father only valued him for what he could do on the farm. His older brother probably achieved more, being older, and this increased the younger's feelings of unworthiness.

Adam and Eve's journey away from the garden began with this same deception. The snake suggested that God was withholding something good from them, that God did not want them to be like him. When they believed that lie, they were separated in their hearts from the source of love. They began to think like orphans who had no father. That inner separation from Abba's love left them feeling empty, so they ate the forbidden fruit.

The Father created them to be like him, to bear his image (Gen.1:26). The serpent convinced them they needed to disregard God's warning to realize their full potential. Believing that lie caused them not only to think like orphans but to act like orphans as well. They disregarded Father's command because they believed he did not love them enough to bring them to fulfillment.

Behavior follows believing, but this believing is not what you reason in your mind or agree with intellectually. We act according to what we feel to be true in our heart. Often, we do not know what is in our heart until someone or some event triggers us. Our response exposes our heart. When we react to a trigger we often say, "I wasn't thinking." It is true. We were not thinking, we were feeling and acting out what we felt in our heart to be true. We are bound by the belief system that is in our heart.

At this point in the story the younger brother has not yet hit bottom. He still feels he can take care of himself without his father's help. The only job he could get was feeding pigs in the field. Pigs were considered unclean animals. Prodigal's journey had so completely separated him from his father that he was willing to live with pigs in the field. He wanted to prove he could make it alone. The idea of going back home did not occur to him. Not yet.

Our Father in heaven really does love us with unconditional love. If we feel otherwise, that proves we are deceived and in bondage. We are orphans in our thinking. In our folly we strive to feel loved and accepted in a place where no real love or acceptance is available. The foreign country is empty and devoid of love. It only offers counterfeits. That is why we always feel the need for more of what we think will meet our need. It never fulfills and never will.

Some people have so much personal strength that they never have to face their real need. They can make it in the foreign land with their own resources. They become more like the owner of the pig farm than the prodigal. They can make it by victimizing others. They will never face their own need until they are broken, and they will not break easily. How sad.

The *reality* of belonging in Father's bosom is much better than the *feeling* of belonging in the foreign country. The bondage of being away from Father's house may feel like freedom at first, but it is not. Likewise, the freedom of being in Father's house can feel like bondage. It seems we humans need to experience the results of real bondage before we are able to recognize true freedom.

We must allow our focus to shift from our feelings to the reality of Father God's love for us. With this shift we can begin to experience freedom as being bound to him by Love.

Prayer

Father, thank you for the love you demonstrated through giving your Son. Help us recognize our bondage and receive the bond of your liberating love.

Part Four

Turning and Returning

What prompted his return? Was it the discomfort and disappointment he was experiencing in the pig pen? Or was the pig pen only the stage on which the inner drama is enacted? I believe it was the latter. Difficult circumstances are often the portal to a better life. But it is not enough to be at the entrance. We must choose to cross over the threshold.

If his heart had not turned toward home, he would never have returned, not even if things got worse. There are many who would rather die than admit they have been wrong. *Inner turning* must precede *returning*. There must be a change of heart. But we are powerless to change our own heart. "Create in me a clean heart, O God," David prayed (Ps. 51:10). David knew it would take an act of God, a miracle from above, to change his heart.

David prayed that prayer only after he had seen things differently, after he repented and acknowledged his wrong. He had been denying it, covering it, and trying to deal with it on his own for quite some time. His denial only brought him into the pit of despair, into the gaping chasm. The prophet Nathan woke him from

79

his dream and set him on the way to reconciliation with himself and with God.

This section is about the inward turn that must precede the spiritual return. Until that inward shift takes place, we can only dream we are on the way to a better life. That inward transformation happens when we see things differently, when we wake up and realize we have been deceiving ourselves by thinking we were doing well.

What was it that woke the prodigal son from his dream?

Reflection Seventeen

A Heart Turned by Love

"But when he came to himself, he said, 'How many of my father's hired Servants have more than enough bread, but I perish here with hunger.'" (Lk 15:17)

He came to himself. That implies he had been away from himself, or beside himself. He was trying to find himself by doing things that were contrary to his birthright. What we call "coming to the end of yourself" is really *coming to your true self.* Your true self cannot make it alone. Your true self needs a helper, a Father. He had not known his true self because he had rejected his father, the source of his nature and his very being.

He separated himself from himself (his true self who needs another) when he withdrew from his father and his family. The geographical separation was a natural result of his inner alienation. All this was because he had not responded to his father's welcoming embrace. Coming to himself, then, implies turning toward home, turning in his heart to the father and his family.

The sheep and the coin also had community. The sheep was part of a flock before the disconnect. A lost sheep is separated from the shepherd, from himself as part of a flock, and from the flock as well. When the coin got detached from the band (community) of ten coins, it lost its connection to the other nine and was no longer identified with the headband.

Here in the pig pen the prodigal turned to his father inwardly before he returned geographically. This turning first took the form of recognizing that his father's servants were better off than he was. He suddenly understood things differently. You will remember the meaning of repentance is to see things differently. The focus at this point was not on the bad things he had done, but on the goodness of his father. This is not self-condemnation.

The father's love had traveled across the hills and valleys to find his son. The son's rejection of the father had not affected the father's goodness, nor had it caused the father to stop loving him. It put the son outside the fellowship of the father's love, outside the family, and away from the house. It also separated him from himself as father's beloved son. But he was never separated from his father's love, not in his father's heart.

When God formed Adam, he said, "Good." When he separated Eve, he said, "Very good!" It was very good because mankind could now function in community, God loved and approved what he made because he made it in his likeness. The Triune Community of the Father, Son and Holy Spirit could now be reflected in the relationship between man and woman (fellowman).

When they turned their hearts from him and ate the forbidden fruit, he did not stop loving them. In fact, that is when he committed himself to send his love (Jesus) to the foreign country outside the 'farm'. In every generation Father's love has been reaching out to Adam's race and experiencing rejection from the majority. God is always asking, "Adam, where are you?" The Bible is a story of God seeking man, not of man seeking God.

The prodigal did not find love; love found the prodigal. His father's love caused him to come to himself. That love was deep inside all along, knocking at the door of his heart and consciousness, crying out for recognition. Withdrawal from Abba does not affect his love for us, but it does affect our relationship with him. No matter how far we stray, his love follows us, inviting us back into his embrace. His love is truly unconditional. His love endures forever.

One clear sign that we have turned is when we 'come to ourselves' and realize we are children of a good Father who loves us and remains for us even after what we have done. We will begin to recognize love where we never saw it before. We will begin to see good in those we thought were disgusting, like the circle of tax collectors and sinners. We will also begin to see ourselves as persons of value and significance. We will experience community again.

Coming to ourselves, and thus turning our hearts to our Father, to the family and the larger community, is the first step to returning home. Abba is waiting.

Prayer

Thank you, Father, for continuing to love us even when we resist you. Help us to recognize and receive the love you sent to us in Jesus Christ.

Reflection Eighteen

The Good Father

"But when he came to himself, he said, 'How many of my father's hired servants have more than enough bread, but I perish here with hunger!'" (Lk. 15:17)

"My father's hired servants have more than enough." Coming to himself involved turning his heart toward his father. He woke up to the fact that his father was a good man. He was good even to his servants. As a matter of fact, his father was extravagantly good to his servants. He was a prodigal father. His servants had *more than enough* of what they needed to have a good life.

The owner of the pig farm was not good to his servants. He did not pay enough to make ends meet nor would he allow them to eat what belonged to his pigs. Life outside the father's house is not as good as the prodigal expected it to be. At home he had never suffered lack, but he did not attribute that to his father's goodness; perhaps he did not even notice. He thought he could do much better on his own.

Nevertheless, the prodigal had felt like he was suffering lack when he was at home. He lacked the opportunity to feed his lust. He lacked the freedom from restrictions that would allow him to do as he pleased. He lacked the feeling of being more important than others. He had felt like he was no different from a slave even though, as a son of the father, he was the owner of the estate. (Gal. 4:1)

Up to the point where he came to himself, the prodigal only remembered his father's house with resentment. As long as his money was still available, he only thought of the freedom to do as he pleased without responsibility. It is likely that the father had tried to teach him to manage servants and land. But he wanted to have exciting experiences. He only saw his father as a barricade keeping him from the good life.

When he came to himself, he suddenly saw the reality of life outside his father's house. Now that he was awake, he began to think of home in a new light. The father's love was still living in the son's memory. He had suppressed that memory because he wanted pleasures that were not available in father's house. He had not acknowledged the truth of his father's love because he took pleasure in unrighteousness (I Thess. 2:12).

His father had given him over to the foreign land in the hope that he would come to himself and return (Rom. 1:24). But the prodigal had suppressed the truth in his desires for pleasure. The father had no choice because a son's love cannot be forced. Love freely given can only wait for a free response from the beloved. Until that response is given in freedom, true love can only wait in hope.

Many of Abba's sons and daughters are in the foreign land and do not recognize the signs of their dissociation from the Father's household. It is like we are in the foreign land waiting for Jesus to return and get us out of this mess while the Father is waiting for us to experience that necessary turn in our heart, the turn back to Father's love. He is the Waiting Father indeed.

Some of us have thought our problem stems from God's unwillingness to come through for us. "Why doesn't God...?" we ask. We think of ourselves as helpless victims who have no resources to get ourselves out of the predicament we are in. That is orphan thinking. We may have been victimized at some point, as the prodigal was by the pig farmer, but remaining a victim is a choice. A bad choice at that.

We are not victims, we are sons. Our Daddy God has all the resources we need, and those resources are available to all who will return to the household and stop trying to make it on their own or stop waiting for him to give what he has already given. With him, in his house, all necessary things are available. There is more than enough for all.

How deep must we go into the chasm before we acknowledge that our Father's house is better than the foreign country?

Prayer

Father, activate the memory of your goodness in our hearts. Help us to see your unconditional love for all mankind. You are waiting for our return.

Reflection Nineteen

Against Heaven

"I will arise and go to my father, and I will say to him, 'Father, I have sinned against heaven and before you.'" (Lk. 15:18)

The decision to return came after coming to himself and recognizing himself to be the son of a good father. With that recognition came a realization of what he had actually done when he divorced his father in his heart. At home he had been so focused on his fantasy of a good life that he was not aware of the good life he already had. We seldom see the seriousness of sin until we meet Abba's love head-on.

In rejecting his father, he had turned from his God-given nature. We are generally not consciously aware of what we are doing when we break away from a father. We are blinded to what we have as a gift from Abba because we are too focused on what we think we want. The hook-and-bait that lures us seems of more value than what God has provided. This is the enemy's deception. He suggests to us that Abba is holding out on us.

Divorcing his father was a sin against love. His father's love came from the Father in heaven; therefore, his sin was against heaven. God is love; any rejection of true love is a rejection of God. Some earthly fathers are not fully able to love freely, yet they do have a measure of love for their sons. Their own childhood wounds may block or contaminate the flow, but true love is there somewhere deep inside because they were created in the image of God.

In the lost sheep and lost coin stories we saw repentance as a willingness to be brought to a party we do not deserve. Repentance here is recognizing the truth of what we have done in the context of who we really are. Repentance begins with coming to ourselves, acknowledging that we are sons and that we belong with our Father in the community of love. Our direction in life will not change until we see ourselves clearly.

We do not see sin as sin until we come to ourselves. We may recognize that there is something wrong with the way our life is going, but we think the end justifies the means. Or we think the misery is some other person's fault. When we are thinking about breaking off a God-given relationship, we might even appeal to God's goodness to justify ourselves. "After all," we think, "God wants me to be happy, he wants me to live a life of pleasure."

"I have sinned against heaven," the prodigal said. Like the prodigal we are more interested in what we want than in fulfilling the Father's design for our life. Abba's purpose for us, our rightful inheritance, is to receive his love and give it away to others, even to those who sin against us. Our selfishness and failure to love unconditionally is primarily a sin against heaven.

Our selfishness is not the real problem, however. Believing that God approves of our selfishness is worse than merely being selfish. Sin is bad, not because it is naughty but because it implies that we believe God either cannot or will not meet our real needs. We act as though God is not good unless he gives us what we want. When we recognize our selfishness as a bad thing, as a sin against love, we are on the way to recovery.

The prodigal's sin was against God, but it was *before* his father. Our sin against the Father's love is in the presence of others. They are affected by our failure to love or by the perverted love we give. By separating ourselves from them, we deprive them of the gift God gave them when he gave us to them. If we have received Father's love, then he gave us to them as his offer of love to them.

Fullness of life does not come without an intimate relationship with Abba. We all know that, at least in our minds. But abundance of life is also tied to intimacy with those God has placed in our circle. Selfishness is a high wall that exalts itself against intimacy (II Cor. 10:5). Self-centeredness draws a circle that keeps others out. Love draws a circle that includes even sinners.

The image of God in man is the image of intimacy. The Father loves the Son and the Son loves the Father in the intimacy of the Holy Spirit. To fail in fellowship is to fail as a human being.

Prayer

Father, help us to acknowledge the others in our life as a gift from your hand. Teach us to respond to them in love as you have loved us.

Reflection Twenty

Seeing Clearly

"I am no longer worthy to be called your son." (Lk. 15:19)

This statement could be read as self-condemnation coming from low self-esteem. Many Christians see themselves as unworthy to be called sons and daughters of Abba Father. This feeling is accompanied by trying to become worthy through Bible reading, prayer, and good deeds. Yet no matter how hard they try, they still feel unworthy. They are more like the elder brother working in the field than theprodigal.

To me this confession sounds more like the fruit of true repentance. The prodigal suddenly saw himself clearly. Because of his pride and selfishness, he had not been behaving as a son and he had dishonored his father by his pursuit of self-centered pleasure. His older brother felt worthy of sonship because of his hard work. He was actually bitter against his father for not recognizing his worthiness.

The prodigal had seen himself as worthy of a son's inheritance when he left. He was confident enough to ask for his portion before his father died. Now he saw the folly of his action. A fool does not deserve to be called a son. One who has spurned his father's love is not worthy of that love. But the father still loved his foolish son; and the prodigal was still his father's son.

The prodigal did not say, "I am no longer a son." He was not denying his sonship, only his right to be *called* a son. He had come to realize the difference between being a son and being called a son. The father had always known the difference. Sonship is not tied to worthiness, but to birth. Likewise, a father's love is not tied to a son's worthiness; a true father's love is tied to the Father who loves.

When he acknowledged his unworthiness to be called a son, he was walking in the light. He was confessing the truth of his self-centeredness and taking responsibility for the alienation. John said, "If we confess our sin, he is faithful and just to forgive our sin and cleanse us of unrighteousness" (I Jn. 1:9). The son who walked away was now in a place to receive forgiveness and cleansing.

Abba holds us in his heart as sons and daughters even when we walk away. When we yearn for the foreign country, he yearns for our return. When we dishonor him by wasting what he gave us, we are still his sons and daughters. He does not withhold love from us when we reject it. He cannot stop loving without ceasing to be God. His love endures forever.

No matter how foolish we become, we are still sons and daughters of our Father. As such we have value and worth, not based on what we do but on the worth and status of our Father. Abba Father has ultimate worth, and his children share that worth. His worth is tied to his love for us. Our worth is also tied to his love for us. If belonging were based on our love for him, we would be in one day and out the next. Our love is not that stable.

When we dishonor him, he does not disown us. His love endures forever. Since children do not cease to be children when they disobey, they continue to have value as sons and daughters even when they are behaving like fools or orphans. Earthly parents who reject their children are not reflecting the love of our Father in heaven.

The Father has every right to disown us when we have dishonored him, but his love will not allow him to reject us. He will never cease to have a place in his heart for us, not even when we walk away from his love and from our own true selves. Our withdrawal wounds the Father's heart. It also puts us in a position of needing continual distractions and counterfeit affection to fill the father-void. But his love remains. His steadfast love endures forever.

As we said earlier, the New Testament word for repentance simply means to see things differently. When we see our situation in the new light of Father's love, we have already turned to the Father in our heart. This inner turning, this new seeing, will always precede and produce a returning.

When we try to return without this inner turn, we have no power to maintain our new commitment. When we try to improve ourselves by our own will and strength, we must sustain our commitment by our own effort. Only as we receive the revelation of Father's love can we change permanently. When that happens, it is not our work but the work of the Savior.

Let us open our hearts to the Father whose heart has never closed to us. Let his love wake us from our dreams.

Prayer

Father, thank you for your commitment to us. Forgive us for our questioning of your goodness. Help us by your Spirit to see things in the light of your love.

Reflection Twenty-One

True Repentance

"Father, I have sinned against heaven and before you. I am no longer worthy to be called your son." (Lk. 15:18-19)

He did not excuse himself. True confession can never take the form of self-justification. Confession can only say, "I was wrong." We add our circumstances to the mix only to save face (a false face at that). When we give excuses for what we have done, we still secretly think we are somehow justified for the wrong we have done. We think we were victimized.

Sometimes we think of our sin as something circumstances did to us rather than our willful action. We think we could have done better under different circumstances. We fail to recognize that we are the ones who need to change, not the circumstances. "If I had it to do over, I would do it differently," we think. We would indeed find another wrong way to do it.

Neither did the prodigal blame the elder brother or the father for the wrong he had done. It may be true that the older brother had rejected him and abused him. But the prodigal was fully and personally at fault in his response to his brother. In his confession he was acknowledging his personal responsibility for his wrong reaction.

He could have excused himself or blamed others only if he had not yet seen his behavior as against Father God. David understood this. When Nathan the prophet exposed his sin with Bathsheba, David wrote, "Against you, you only, have I sinned and done what is evil in your sight" (Ps. 51:4). Bathsheba and her husband had certainly been violated, but the sin was ultimately against the love of Abba Father, against heaven.

As long as we think our negative responses to people are primarily against them, we have not yet seen clearly what we have done, we have not yet truly repented. We have not yet come to ourselves if we excuse ourselves because they "deserve" our rejection. Whether we deal with it by denial, excusing ourselves or blaming others, we are still disconnected from ourselves and from God. We will not reconnect until we see our action in relation to Father God's love.

The suffering we cause others when we sin against them will never wound them as deeply as it has wounded our Father God. The Father suffered at Calvary as much as his Son did. Long before others feel the pain of what we have done, and long before we feel sorry, Abba has already felt the pain and experienced the anguish. Before we even realize what we have done, the Father and the Son have already willingly absorbed that shock and more at the cross.

The real damage caused by sin appears at the Cross. Man's sin wrecked the relationship between God and his creation. Mankind rejected God at the cross. Because the Son had become a man, our sin also wrecked the relationship between the Father and the Son, Abba had to forsake his beloved Son because of our sin (Matt. 27:46). Father was able to repair that wreckage by the Resurrection, but that does not change what we did.

That tragedy in the life of the Triune God is a windfall for us. When we see Jesus on the cross, we see the extent of Father's love for us and his willingness to carry it all without rejecting us. We see his manifest glory there on the cross. The glory of God is the glory of his unconditional love.

When we violate any human relationship, we disrespect the love which Father God demonstrated at the cross. We fail to reflect the glory of God displayed in Jesus' self-denial. Paul defined sin as falling short of the glory of God (Rom. 3:23). When we do damage to one of Father's beloved, we fail to mirror his glory, we fall short of his glory and we sin against love.

One of the amazing things about the confession, "I have sinned against heaven", is that it becomes a testimony to the unconditional love of Abba Father. When we come to ourselves and make that confession, we are throwing ourselves into the hands of a loving and merciful God. That act is the ultimate testimony to the glory of God. He accepts us in our failure. His steadfast love endures forever.

His love is wider than the ocean, deeper than the sea, and he is willing to suffer even beyond time. When we see our sin with his love as the backdrop, we have finally repented.

Prayer

Father, your love is amazing, and your grace is more than enough. Help us to see the depth of the love we spurn when we sin.

Reflection Twenty-Two

Sons as Servants

"Treat me as one of your hired servants." (Lk. 15:19)

He did not say, "Make me a hired servant." He was a son, and he knew it. He could never be a hired servant, but he was willing to be treated like one just to be a part of the Father's household. Having his father's provision was more important at this point than status and privilege. His motive was simply to be in a place where food and lodging were available.

His plan to request a servant's position, however, indicates he thought his father would not receive him as a son. As the drama unfolds, we will see that the prodigal did not yet recognize the full extent of his father's goodness. He did not believe a father could actually be good enough to receive one who spurned his love. That will come when he experiences his father's embrace.

The son's willingness to serve in his father's house is not totally out of order. Jesus is the supreme example of true sonship. He did not count equality with God a thing to be grasped. He knew he was the Son but did not presume upon that position. He made himself nothing, taking the form of a servant. He was willing to serve in his Father's house with the full knowledge of his sonship (Phil. 2:6-7).

A true son is willing to serve in his father's house, but he is not a hired hand. A son working in his father's house feeling like a hireling has failed to take his sonship seriously. The prodigal was willing to join the elder brother in the field as hired help because he also believed he had to earn access to his father's provision. When we believe admission to our Father's presence is based on our service, we are thinking like orphans and employees.

Jesus' obedience took the form of doing only what he saw his Father doing (Jn. 5:19). A hired servant does what he is told to do. It is his duty. A son does what he sees the Father doing; it is an act that issues from an intimate relationship of love. Hired servants focus on the household tasks; sons focus on the Father of the household. With attention centered on the Father, intimacy develops, and a son has a place near the Father where he can sense his heart, not merely hear his commands.

Our culture does not see intimacy as tied to obedience. When we try to become intimate with Abba today, sometimes our interest in Father's embrace is all about the good feeling of being embraced. It is all about us. True biblical intimacy comes through being intimately connected to Abba Father's heart for others. If we are tied into his heart, we will automatically produce fruit for his kingdom; we will do the things that reveal his heart to those around us. That is biblical obedience issuing from intimacy.

In his obedience, Jesus was not trying to earn a place in his Father's heart. He knew he was in the Father and that the Father was in him (Jn. 14:11). Obedience for him was a response to his Father's love for the world. His Father's love constrained him (II Cor. 5:14). We demonstrate true sonship when we are constrained by the Father's love for us and allow his love to flow through us to the world around us.

We mentioned above that the prodigal had not yet realized the magnitude of his father's goodness. He still thought he needed to do something to have a place in his father's house. His desire to serve his father was not based on the father's goodness but on his own personal need for care and provision. He will not grasp the extent of his father's love until he acts on his decision to return.

Many of us today fail to experience Father's embrace for the same reason. We are convinced we must do something to earn Abba's acceptance. We think we must deal with our own sin before he will make the full extent of his love available to us. We forget that he already made his love available when he sent Jesus into the world to save sinners.

How much of our obedience is based on our need for care and provision? How much is really motivated by the Father's love for others?

Prayer

Father, thank you for your goodness. Help us to experience the life of true obedience by simply responding to your love. Bring us into maturity as sons and daughters.

Reflection Twenty-Three

Arise and Go

"And he arose and came to his father." (Lk. 15:20)

Turning inwardly to the Father is never the end. We must also arise and go. If the inner turning is genuine, arising and going will follow as a matter of course. If we are still wallowing in self-pity or self-condemnation, we are still self-focused. We may wish things were different and we may long for comfort and provision, but that is not the same thing as turning and returning.

I once heard someone say, "God knows where I am. If he wants me, he knows where to find me." The first part is true. God knows where we are. But the "if" implies that he might not want me involved in what he is doing. That is an insult to his love. He came to us with his love in the person of his Son. In that act he demonstrated the depth of his love and his desire to involve us in his coming kingdom.

"He knows where to find me" implied that it was God's responsibility to seek us. That person's heart had not yet turned.

The prodigal did not wait for his father to come to the pigsty. He arose and went to his father. The lost sheep and the lost coin contributed nothing to their return, but the one who came to himself knew the value of a relationship with his dad, so he arose and went. The diligence of the woman seeking the lost coin comes to mind here. We have a part to play in our returning to Father.

Before his inner turn the prodigal might have thought, "If my father loved me, he would come take me out of this mess. He knows where I am." His father probably did know where he was. But when he came to himself, the son realized he was the one who needed to make a move. His father's original move toward his son was still in effect. The father never changed his mind about his son. Like in a chess game, Father has moved; it is your turn to move.

Jesus, the Son who is telling this story, wants us to know that our Father has not changed his mind about us. When he created Adam, he created what he wanted, and he wanted what he created. He said, "very good" (Gen. 1:31). He loved his creatures, and he has not changed his mind. He proved his love on Calvary. What more could he do?

The inward turning takes the form of seeing things differently, as we have said. It takes the form of recognizing we have believed a lie. What does it take for us to come to ourselves? It takes a jolt, an experience of such proportions that it shocks us back into reality. In a word, it takes a revelation of Father's love. The cross of Jesus was designed to accomplish just that.

When we see him on the cross, we notice that we are even willing to kill God to maintain ourselves in the lie. Even seeing his death may not be enough to cause us to turn. If we still think of God as a harsh taskmaster, we will rejoice at the death of his Son because we can now take over the estate and run things our way. There is a parable about that (Matt. 21:33-39).

Jesus showed us the full extent of Father's love by submitting to our violence against him. As long as we see the cross of Jesus only as a sacrifice to an angry God, we will not have the ability to repent. When we see it as a murder we committed (Acts 3:15), the truth begins to dawn. The light shines brightly through the resurrection when Jesus returns to give grace for those who murdered him.

Even to this day he is still submitting to Adam's violence against himself. (He has not consumed the world with fire yet.) He is still patiently waiting for us to come to ourselves and catch sight of Father's unconditional love. Abba gave his most precious possession to woo us to himself. He sent his Son because he wanted to bring many sons and daughters to glory (Heb. 2:10). That is us. We are the ones he wants to bring to his party.

He loves us, O, how he loves us. Let us rise and return to Father's bosom.

When we see (really see) his unconditional commitment to us, we are stirred and empowered to rise and go to the Father. This is seeing things differently. This is repentance.

Prayer

Father, thank you that you did not abandon us when we rejected you. Open our eyes to see your fatherhood in the light of the death and resurrection of Jesus.

Part Five

Father's Embrace

Finally, we come to the geographical return to the father's house. There has been the inner turning prompted by the abiding memory of his father's goodness. That turning took the form of coming to himself. Now he turns outwardly to the father's house; he is going to his father.

The Old Testament word for repentance implies a change of direction. Even in that time, however, the mere outward returning was not enough. The people often turned to the Lord in times of trouble only to return to their old ways as soon as the problem was removed. Their turning was in pretense only. It was not the kind of turning needed for reconciliation, because their heart remained the same.

Father has always wanted a circumcised heart, a heart where the desire to go our own way has been cut away. It is this inward turn he is after. He knows the outward turn will certainly follow.

When the prodigal went to the foreign land, he found less than he expected. When he returned to his father, he found more than he expected. He anticipated a reception that would include a job in the field with his brother or a position as a household servant. He was willing to take that position to have his needs met.

He never dreamed his father would embrace him and restore him to full fellowship before he earned it. The idea of his father giving him a new robe, scandals, and the signet ring did not occur to him. It never entered his mind that the fatted calf would become a banquet meal to honor his return.

Reflection Twenty-Four

No Condemnation

"But while he was still a long way off, his father saw him, felt compassion, and ran to embrace him and kissed him. The son said to him, "Father, I have sinned against heaven and before you. I am no longer worthy to be called your son." (Lk 15:20)

The father ran. There was no hesitation when he saw his son at a distance. He did not wait for an apology or admission of regret or guilt. After years of yearning for his son's presence, he could not restrain his enthusiasm. He embraced his son and kissed him. He was not ashamed of this son despite the way the son had dishonored him.

The son was not distracted by his father's public display of affection. He hurried to give his prepared speech. He was not aware that his confession would not be necessary. He had come to himself and realized he had a good father, but he was not yet aware of how exceptionally good his father was. Nor was he fully aware of his own privileges as a son of this father. He still felt the need to give his speech and ask for a servant's position.

The condemnation prompting his speech was not coming from his father. He had not realized the significance of the fact that his father ran out to meet him. His father's embrace had not yet landed in his heart. He still felt compelled to make his "I'm-sorry-let-me-be-a-servant" speech. The speech originated in his own self-condemnation.

As we noticed earlier, he was willing to join the elder brother in the field as a hired servant for the privilege of having a comfortable place to sleep and food to eat. He knew his father was good to his servants, but he still felt unworthy to be called a son. "*Worthiness must be earned by sons*," was the lie he believed; the same lie elder brother believed.

Much like the prodigal, once we return to Abba, we feel obliged to experience prolonged self-condemnation. We feel we must let Father know how terrible we have been and how sorry we are. We forget that Jesus was sent to save, not to condemn the world. Like the prodigal, we do not know how good our Father really is.

I wonder how his father would have responded if the prodigal had continued to berate and degrade himself after he had received him. The father's joy would have been squelched if the son did not receive his welcoming arms. Our Father's joy is also quenched when we do not accept his embrace.

That is an amazing thought—that we can affect Abba Father in this way; we can grieve him. Paul would not have admonished us to "quench not the Spirit" if it were not possible to do so (I

Thess. 5:19). The other side of this is that we also fail to enter the joy ourselves when we wallow in self-condemnation. When we wallow, we are suffering by our own hands.

Our Father does not join us in our self-judgment. He has already prepared a party for us in his presence; celebration and feasting are waiting for us when we accept the invitation to intimacy. But, if we are still condemning ourselves, we are still outside the house. We are with the Father, the father is with us, but we are outside the place where the joy of intimacy awaits—in Father's bosom.

In the parable the father came out of his house to meet his returning son. Our Father also came out of his house in the person of his Son to get our attention and to make a way for us to return. His unconditional love for the world prompted him to leave his house while we were still a long way off.

That same love—his love—stirred us earlier when we came to ourselves. It was his love for us in both cases. His love moved him to act in our behalf, and his love set our heart in motion to return. It will be his love that overcomes our self-focus as well. As long as we are trying to become worthy of his affection, we will continue to fall short.

The more we receive the unmerited embrace of Father, the more we enter into the joy of life with him. How can we do otherwise when we see him rejoicing over us?

Prayer

Father, thank you for your open arms. Help us to accept your welcome and stop trying to convince you we are not worthy.

Reflection Twenty-Five

Received as a Son

"But the father said to his servants, 'Bring quickly the best robe, and put it on him, and put a ring on his hand, and shoes on his feet." (Luke 15:22)

The father interrupted the son's prepared speech. He may have sensed that the son was about to ask for a servant's position. He would not hear of it; he would not allow it. This was his son. He chose to honor him and give him the favor and blessing appropriate to sonship. The father received him back with no condemnation and with no demand for restitution of the wasted inheritance.

When we return, having seen things differently, Abba Father does not have a long list of things to get straight before he receives us back. He knows our heart better than we know ourselves. He will begin restoring us to full sonship as soon as we arrive. Our heart will be changed from stone to flesh by seeing the depth and breadth of Father's love. There are no hoops to jump through to belong in this household.

The prodigal's father called his servants to minister to his son. This reminds me of the story of Lazarus. After raising him from the dead, Jesus said to those who were witnesses, "Unbind him, and let him go" (Jn. 11: 44). We are all servants—sons of the Father—and we are called to minister to those who are returning to him from the grave of the foreign country. We are neither judges nor executioners. We are ministers of his love.

Once the father saw his son's heart had turned, he knew he was ready to receive status and authority within the household. He gave this in three ways.

The best robe is a symbol of highest dignity. Our Father replaces our shame with the robe of righteousness. Jesus himself is our righteous robe. Father made Christ Jesus to be "our wisdom and our righteousness and sanctification and redemption" (I Cor. 1:30). In him we have become the righteousness of God in Christ. You cannot get any more righteous than that (II Cor. 5:21).

The ring was probably a signet ring, giving the son authority within the household and the estate. This gave the son access to the treasures as well as authority to do the work of the father. This is the authority Jesus exercised in the days of his flesh. In his humanity he exercised this authority by doing only what he saw the Father doing (Jn. 5:19). That same authority has been given to us. He brought us out of the pigsty into a place of authority in Father's house.

The shoes on the feet speak of our ability to walk uprightly in the presence of Father and before men. Our Father gives these shoes to every son or daughter who returns from the foreign land. These shoes are not given to orphans, slaves, or to sons who act like slaves. We have received the Spirit of Sonship (Rom. 8:14-17). Paul encouraged us in this way, "...walk by the Spirit and you will not gratify the desires of the flesh" (Gal. :16).

The younger brother must have been shocked, even stunned and flabbergasted, by his father's extravagant and generous response to his return. He was expecting a servant's position at best. But his father lavished his love on him with these honors. At this point the truth of his father's goodness began to dawn on him. With the signet ring the son who wasted his inheritance now has access to the whole estate.

Our Father replaced our shame with his dignity. He replaced our weakness with his authority. He wants us to have everything we need to carry on the business of his household. So, he enabled us to walk by the Spirit. He did all this through Jesus on the cross, and he made it available to us by the Spirit after the resurrection. We see things differently when we realize that "Christ died for the ungodly" (Rom. 5:6). That is me. I qualify.

Now we see it all as a gift of his grace. He is not waiting for us to deserve it. All we have to do to qualify for the Father's embrace is to be an 'ungodly sinner' who sees things differently. That is who he died for and that is who he lives for. We sing a song, "It's all about you...." He sings that same song over you and me. He sings. "Jesus on the cross is all about you," as he reaches out his arms to embrace us. Father is waiting for our return. His love endures forever.

117

Kingdom authority is given to those who receive it as a gift. It cannot be earned.

Prayer

Father, thank you for your free gift. Help us receive it freely without feeling we must deserve it—without thinking we might miss it because of what we have or have not done.

Reflection Twenty-Six

The Fellowship Meal

"And bring the fattened calf and kill it and let us eat and celebrate." (Lk. 15:23)

In that culture every farmer had a calf in a stall being fed a special diet designed to produce the best meat available for celebration. The fatted calf is generally related to the sacrifice called a peace offering or fellowship offering. When this animal was slaughtered, the meat was cooked and family, friends, and guests were invited to partake of this covenant meal. In this way they celebrated their relationship.

Jesus is our peace offering. Paul wrote, *"He is our peace (offering), who has broken down in his flesh the dividing wall of hostility"* (Eph. 2:14). Through him we have access to the Father (Eph. 2:18). So, the fatted calf is all about the celebration of a relationship. Celebration does not come before reconciliation if there has been a breach. Celebration comes on the heels of the inner turning, the arising, and the return of the separated one.

It is evident from the end of this story that the father prepared the covenant meal for both brothers. But the elder brother did not come to the party. He refused to be a part of the reconciliation. His real condition did not come into view until the prodigal returned home. The servants probably thought he was okay with his father, but he was very much in need of reconciliation with his brother and with his father. He needed an inner turning.

It was in the context of the covenant meal that Paul said, "Consider the people of Israel; are not those who eat the sacrifices participants in the altar?" (1 Cor. 10:18). This meal means we are participating in the peaceful life of the Father as a part of the house. We claim to be partners in the altar when we chose to partake of the meal. By eating this meal, we proclaim our participation in the life of the Father as a part of the household of God. We are celebrating our peaceful relationship with the Father of the house and with his family.

Concerning this covenant meal Paul also gave a warning. "Whoever, therefore, eats the bread or drinks the cup of the Lord in an unworthy manner will be guilty of profaning the body and blood of the Lord" (I Cor. 11:27). The phrase "participants in the altar" implies a mutual relationship with the God of the altar and with all who participate in the celebration. The elder brother would refuse to be a partner in the father's altar.

Partaking of the external sign has no value if we are not in fellowship. If there is animosity toward others at the table, eating together is a mockery. The "unworthy manner" refers to eating the meal while avoiding intimacy with others at the table. To eat this covenant meal while resenting someone at table with the

Father is to fail in your fellowship with the Father of the household. You are refusing to love one whom the Father loves.

This parable was Jesus' response to the Pharisees criticism of him for eating with sinners. In that culture when people ate together that implied there was covenant fellowship between those gathered around the table. The Pharisees were scandalized by the fact that Jesus had covenant fellowship with sinners, and openly proclaimed it by eating with them. They refused to eat a meal with Jesus and his questionable friends.

Those religious leaders must have been shocked and shaken at this turn in the story. To share a meal with someone before they have cleaned up their act was outrageous and offensive to their understanding of holiness. To them God was so holy his presence would consume anyone who did not live a holy life. They kept their distance lest they die. They did not realize he wanted to consume their iniquity without consuming them.

Like the sinners who were at ease eating with Jesus, the prodigal was also comfortable entering the celebration. They were all relaxed for the same reason, they knew they were accepted and loved in spite of their weaknesses and failures. We are allowed to celebrate our relationship with Abba on the same basis. We are loved and accepted by him even though we do not do everything right. His love is unconditional. His love endures forever.

It is not the elder brother (or the Pharisees), but the father, who invites the guests. Will you come when he invites tax collec-

tors and sinners to the table? Will you fellowship with sinners? Is your heart as open as Abba Father's heart?

Prayer

Thank you, Father, that you have invited us to the table. Help us to be open to the other sinners you have invited to the celebration.

Reflection Twenty-Seven

Identified with Christ

"For this my son was dead, and is alive again; he was lost, and is found." (Luke 15:24)

The prodigal son was "dead in sin," but now he is alive. He was lost to himself, to his father and to the whole family of those who were intimate with his father, but now he is found. The father found his son. He had not gone out looking for him, but he had sent his love to the foreign country to find him and bring him back home.

Most of us can identify with the prodigal. We were dead in the trespasses and sins in which we once walked (Eph. 2:1-2). We were not aware we were dead until he gave us life. We thought we were more alive than those who were limited by their commitment to Jesus. Those who are not aware of their lost condition have not come to themselves. Revelation breaks in, we suddenly see things differently, and we realize we have been dead, alienated from the Source of life. We are alive again.

But there is another death. Even after we are born again, we continue to experience a daily dying to our old ways, daily turning and returning to the Father, "again for the first time," we might say. Our inner nature is being renewed day by day (II Cor. 4:16) as we take up our cross daily to follow him. The cross is not a burden to bear, it is an execution instrument. It is a place to die to old behavior patterns, whether from the foreign land or from the field, and come alive to new life in Father's house.

Jesus died so we could be identified with his death. His death was a death to sin. My self-life was crucified with Christ Jesus (Rom. 6:1-6). This is sometimes difficult to understand. Think of it like this: He was wounded (by us) and we were healed; he was rejected (by us) and we were accepted; he received the death penalty (from us) and we received abundant life.

He was "delivered up because of our trespasses and raised for our justification" (Rom. 4.25). He was raised so we could receive his new life. The word justification is a law court term which could be translated acquittal. When Jesus, the murdered victim, showed up in the courtroom alive, we were acquitted (since no dead body could be presented to prove that we killed him). Our act of murder was ineffective. We are not guilty, because he is alive forevermore. His love endures forever.

The prodigal in this story is also a picture of Jesus coming to our far country to carry our tormented life to the grave. He was prodigal in the sense of recklessly extravagant. He did not only take our sins; he took us with him on his shoulders as he returned home to his father. We died with him, we were buried with him and, when this Prodigal Son of our Prodigal God was received into the joyful life of his Father's house, we were raised with him into a new life with his Father (Rom. 6:1-4).

He is the robe of righteousness we receive as we approach the celebration; he is the robe we wear to the feast. He is the signet ring on our finger. He gave us authority to do "kingdom business" in his name. He is the sandals on our feet, securing our walk in the presence of Father and in the presence of our enemy. It is no longer I who live (walk) but Christ who lives in me (Gal 2:20).

We represent him as ambassadors in this foreign country (II Cor. 5:19-20). He called us out of the foreign country to send us back as ambassadors. He gave us the ministry of reconciliation; our commission is to be his mouthpiece in the earth. When we say to the world, "Be reconciled to God," it is Father God himself speaking through us. He sent us into the highways and byways to call others to the celebration. He wants a full house at his party.

In a sense, the Father was at home and in the foreign land at the same time since his love arrived there. We are also at the party and in the foreign country at the same time. We are already seated with him in heavenly places (Eph. 2:6) and from that position we call to those who are in the pigsty and to those in the field, "Come home. Father is not angry with you. He loves you with everlasting love. There is a celebration waiting for you." His love endures forever.

Let us learn to accept our real identity in Christ and behave accordingly.

Prayer

Father, thank you for your open arms, open even to us who have rejected your Son. Empower us to be effective ambassadors of your love here where we are now.

Part Six

The Elder Brother

Now we turn our attention to the elder brother. The father had divided the property between the sons, yet this son was still living as though he were a hired hand. He continued to work in the field trying to gain enough favor with his father to have a party in the house with his friends. It is as though he did not know the house belonged to him. It was his house.

The elder brother syndrome is not limited to religion. You can find them everywhere. You will find them in homes, in offices, in schools, and in many other walks of life. You can recognize them because they are always right in their own eyes and feel a need to prosecute anyone who does not measure up to their standards. They feel a need to attack any who disagree with them.

They are always playing one-upmanship, even with people who do not care about status or position. Their need to feel superior drives them to put others down. For them it is not enough to be right, they must prove others wrong. It is as though the only way they feel good about themselves is to put others in a bad light. "For me to be right, you have to be wrong," is their motto. And they must be right.

Finally, they are always busy, always striving for higher positions. Someone described this performance orientation perfectly when he said, "I climbed the corporate ladder all the way to the top and discovered it was leaning against the wrong building." That is the life of elder brothers.

As we consider the elder brother in the parable, we will be on the lookout for reasons why he had to put others down and stay busy to feel right. Watch for pride, superiority, bitterness, and hidden anger.

Reflection Twenty-Eight

The Busyness Bond

"Now his older son was in the field, and as he came and drew near to the house, he heard music and dancing." (Lk. 15:25)

The elder son was not coming to the house because his brother was home. He was finished with his duty for the day. Because of his busyness he was not even aware a party was in progress. Busyness tends to keep us from noticing other people except as they relate to what we are doing. We only become aware of others as we notice they are either useful or useless. There can be no intimacy with busyness.

As the elder brother was drawing near, he heard music and dancing. He probably thought, "What a waste of time. These people should be doing something worthwhile." This son was so focused on achievement that he saw no value in festivity. Celebration requires time for preparation. That time could be used more productively. Celebration also cost money. To the elder son it is a waste because his standard is productivity rather than relationship.

The elder brother never left home, but he had never really been at home either. He was like hired help on his father's farm. He had so identified with his work ethic that it had become a bondage to him. It was a burden on his shoulders he was not free to unload because he was compelled to stay busy and productive enough to feel good about himself. But it was not working. He may not have been aware of it, but he was miserable.

When we orient our lives totally around productivity and achievement, our emotions become blocked. We cannot feel our pain, we cannot feel our increasing misery, and we cannot feel joy either. We just grit our teeth and do what must be done. We are driven. We even lose track of why we are working so hard (Eccl. 4:8). We are unaware that life is passing by and we are missing it. But we feel no loss. We feel nothing—except anger.

Perhaps the greater tragedy is that we also fail to feel the joy and pain of others. Our focus on obligations keeps us from joining others in their party or in their misery. It keeps us from standing as a support for those who are experiencing difficult times. Our concentration on duty is a barrier to any real relationship. Busyness blocks intimacy and leaves us alone and lonely.

This condition is like being frozen in a time warp without any memory of why we are there and no awareness that things could be different. We are in bondage to our busyness. We cannot break the chains because we do not even feel their grip on us. We think that is just the way life is. We have no hope of a better life. Life becomes a nightmare of running and getting nowhere.

All this is a result of a failure to receive the love that is abundantly and freely available from Abba Father. Trying to earn significance through activity keeps us out of the peaceful and welcoming presence of a Father who loves us as much as he loves the prodigals who have returned. The reason we do not feel loved is that we do not feel anything.

The elder brother was drawing near to the house, but he was not coming home to his father. He was not coming to the party; he was only drawing near to the house. *Drawing near, always drawing near, but never arriving.* He was too preoccupied to notice he never entered. He felt like he had not yet done enough work outside the house.

That is a picture of all who strive to earn a right to a party by working for Abba Father rather than relating to him. Like the Pharisees, they don their religious robes and embellish them with many good deeds. Then they parade themselves before others as prime examples of righteousness and they disdain those who are less righteous. But they are outside the house just as those who admire them are.

The field of busyness is just as far from home as the foreign country, perhaps farther. Come home to Abba. He will give you rest.

Prayer

Thank you, Abba, for your welcoming arms. Help us to break free from busyness bondage and come home.

Reflection Twenty-Nine

The Bitterness Bond

"*And he called one of the servants and asked what these things meant.*" (Luke. 15:26)

Why did he not go into the house and ask his father? This son related better to the servants than he did to his father. Perhaps it was because he knew he had a superior position to all the servants. He was a son of the owner; in fact, he was the owner. But he apparently had trouble relating to people who were equal (like his brother) or above him (like his father). He needed a superior position before he could relate.

From a superior position he could give commands and make demands with no obligation to care about the others' feelings. That is the world's concept of superiority. His father was in fact superior to him. The father's positional superiority was in the fact that he was the father, but the superiority of his father's character was expressed by his willingness to love those who were below him, even those who rejected him. He remained open when the other was closed. His steadfast love endures forever.

The elder's need to appear superior caused him to avoid his father's presence. We will see later that he was harboring resentment because his father had never allowed him to have a party with his friends. He had believed the lie that he had to work for the right to have a party in his own house. Some form of bitterness always enters the heart when we believe the enemy's lie.

When we bury bitterness inside, we erect high walls to keep others from seeing our rancid heart. These walls also keep us on the outside of other people's lives. We usually blame others for the breach in relationship to avoid facing our own decadence. Apparently, the elder brother blamed his father for the rift. Even if others want to relate to us, as the father wanted to relate to this son, they are unable to scale the protective walls we have constructed.

Intimacy is impossible where there are walls that separate. You cannot be intimate with someone on the other side of a wall. The father was not keeping this older son out of the house. The son had chosen to remain outside. He preferred that to the pain of facing his failure to find approval in his father's eyes. He never looked in his father's eyes to see the acceptance that was there. He had to see the father as the bad guy to maintain his feeling of superiority.

Both these elements—the need to appear superior and bitterness—contribute to dysfunctional relationships. We try to control others when we feel superior. If the other holds a superior position, we try to manipulate him or her. One who manipulates assumes his way is superior. In both cases it is the feeling of superiority that tries to control. No one likes to be manipulated or controlled. A dominating spirit blocks intimacy.

This superior feeling expresses itself in many ways. Some people prefer to demand rather than ask for a favor. To ask for a favor is to take an under position. To stay in control, we prefer to demand compliance or ensure compliance by coercing or making the other feel guilty or obligated. We even try to obligate God by our religious activities. To ask for a favor is to leave the response in the hands of the other. That puts us at their mercy.

Some people want to manipulate leaders without taking responsibility for what results from their influence. Manipulators want to make others responsible for making everything work out. That way they will not be blamed if the project fails. They are convinced their way is right but, if things do not go well, it is the leader's failure and they are off the hook. Thus, they maintain their feeling of superiority even when their way causes failure.

Our Father really does know the best way, but he does not manipulate or force us to go his way. He invites us into his way, and he welcomes us if we choose to respond. But he does not coerce. Love does not insist on its own way (I Cor. 13:5). Since God is love, he cannot control or manipulate us without ceasing to be Love, without ceasing to be God. He cannot do that.

The greatest in the kingdom is the servant of all. Let us all strive to maintain the attitude of a servant/son of LOVE.

Prayer

Father, thank you for receiving us even when we behave like the enemy. Help us to be aware of our actions and responses so that we can reflect your love to others.

Reflection Thirty

Work or Pleasure

"Your brother has come, and your father has killed the fatted calf, because he has received him back safe and sound." (Lk. 15:27)

"Your brother is home." That could have been good news if little brother cameback to help on the farm. With his brother helping, much more work could be done each day. With more being accomplished, perhaps the father would finally recognize what value the elder son brought to the work force. The elder would also be able to demonstrate his leadership by making the younger work hard.

In fact, the prodigal *had* come home to work. He was willing to face his big brother again to have the security of his father's house. But the father did not put him to work; he threw a party to celebrate his return. The prodigal allowed himself to be taken into this party he did not deserve.

Big brother's attitude may have been one reason the younger left home to begin with. It is difficult to work under a leader who keeps you in an inferior position so he can feel good about himself. Little brother may have tried to enjoy his work in the field by playing around. Some people can accomplish a lot while enjoying their work. The presence of joy creates a very pleasant environment for work.

When we think of the merriment in the house, we see that the father knew how to enjoy life even though there was work that needed to be done. But for the elder brother, festivity had to be postponed until all the work was done. On a farm the work is never done. There is always something else that needs attention. So, there is no time for celebration.

The younger brother may have enjoyed time with his father before he was old enough to work in the field. When he did come to the field, his elder brother (the Pharisee) may have given him a hard time, using the father's authority (God) as leverage. After several seasons of this, the younger may have concluded that it was the Father (God) who was demanding more work. This may be part of the reason he left.

The elder brother probably had the same desires for pleasure as the younger. He just did not have enough courage to relax like the prodigal did. He probably judged and condemned his brother for doing what he secretly wanted to do. In that way he avoided facing his own inordinate desires. This judgmental attitude also helped the elder feel more righteous than his brother.

Big brother stayed on the farm but was never at home. He continually pressured himself to be more productive. He may have thought he wanted intimacy with his father. If he did, it was only to be on his good side so he could have a party with his friends. He did not want his father, he wanted what his father could provide. That is not intimacy. It is the same attitude that prompted little brother to demand his portion of the inheritance and leave.

Many of us vacillate between these two ways of seeking intimacy. We work hard to earn it until we are tired and weary. The expected intimacy pay-off never comes, so we try to find counterfeit intimacy through pleasure. We focus on pleasure until we feel guilty, then we go back to work trying to accomplish enough to fill the void. In both cases, true intimacy does not follow. *The father-void remains.*

In both cases it is all about our personal productivity or our personal pleasure. But true intimacy is always about the beloved, not about the self. We fail to seek the only thing that can truly satisfy—Abba Father's loving embrace. Or we seek his embrace only to feel good about ourselves. Ultimate delight comes from recognizing and appreciating how good our Abba Father is. When we pursue him simply because he is good, we find joy and satisfaction and we really feel good. But to pursue good feelings for the sake of good feelings is to chase after a lesser pleasure.

The returning prodigal found true intimacy with his father. This new relationship was not based on his willingness to work. It was the fruit of receiving the welcoming embrace of his father. The elder brother missed it. If you are outside the house, it does not matter whether you are in the field or in the foreign country. You have no intimacy with the Father.

Abba Father desires to enjoy our presence.

His work can only be done in his joyful presence. Let us join the party and allow him to take responsibility for the work.

Prayer

Father, we acknowledge our tendency to focus on ourselves. Circumcise our hearts as you draw us close to your bosom.

Reflection Thirty-One

The Father's Entreaty

"But he was angry and refused to go in. His father came out and entreated him..." (Luke 15:28)

The anger of the elder brother betrayed him. He could no longer hide the fact that he resented his father. Who knows how long this bitterness had been brewing in his heart? Perhaps he refused to go in because he feared he might lose his composure and expose his antagonism. It is amazing to what lengths we go to avoid being seen for who we really are!

The father he had was not the kind of father he wanted. He wanted a father who catered to his pride, who would acknowledge his superiority. He longed for everyone, including his father, to recognize his pre-eminence and submit to his demands. It is obvious he was not interested in intimacy with his father, otherwise he would have spent more time in the house enjoying a friendship with him.

He thought he deserved much more than his father was giving him. His focus on earning the favor blinded him to the fact that the house had already been given, it belonged to him as a son. He wanted to be recognized as worthy because of his good works. Grace is undeserved. If anyone gets what they deserve, it is not grace they receive. The younger brother had come to the truth about himself; he knew he did not deserve anything from his father. He had to trust his father's grace and mercy.

The father came out to entreat the elder. Earlier he left his house to greet the returning prodigal. This time he left the merrymaking to plead with the son who had been around the house all along, around but never at home. The father demonstrated his humility in the face of his son's pride. The father's love for his son would not allow him to take advantage of his superior position. Love does not play one-upmanship.

Our Father will also entreat us. The God of heaven and earth is willing to plead with us. Wow! He came out of his house in the person of Jesus Christ to appeal to us, inviting us to boldly enter the Holy of Holies and enjoy his presence. He desires to bring many sons to glory (Heb. 2:10). The basic desire of fatherhood is to have a house full of children who look like their Father, who reflect their Father's glory.

Intimacy with Abba, however, does not exclude work. Jesus said, "the Father is in me doing his work." He did only what he saw the Father doing. If anyone saw Jesus doing something, it was what Father was doing (Jn. 5:19; 14:10). When Jesus welcomed sinners into his presence, it was because his Father was welcoming sinners. When he appealed to the Pharisees, Father was making his appeal through him. Father wants intimacy with all of us. He will not stop calling sinners until his banquet hall is full, and his hall is big enough for the whole world with every generation.

Jesus also said, "I go to prepare a place for you" (Jn. 14:2). That place is in his Father's banquet hall, it is in the bosom of his Father. Jesus is himself the Father's invitation to intimacy. He is the way to the Father (Jn. 14:6). When we limit the meaning of this verse to 'heaven someday', we miss the real point. Abba wants to be our friend here and now. He wants to spend time with us again today. He wants to enjoy our presence here.

But elder brothers do not want a God who desires to be a friend and do things together. They want one who will acknowledge their ability to accomplish things without his help. They want recognition for being sufficient unto themselves, for having the ability to manage the farm on their own. Like Little Jack Horner in the nursery rhyme, they want Father to admit they have done an awesome thing when they pull their thumb out of the pie with a plumb on it.

When we complain and grumble about what God has not done, we expose the fact that we are not satisfied with God as he is. We want him to change to fit our image of what he ought to be. We secretly worship another god. This is the same prideful attitude the elder brother had.

Being exposed in our selfishness is a good thing if it prompts us to deal with it. We will not enter the house and enjoy the party until we acknowledge we do not deserve it.

Prayer

Father, help us deal with our self-centeredness so we can accept your invitation to intimacy. We really want to be with you as friend with friend.

Reflection Thirty-Two

Receiving the Inheritance

"Look, these many years I have served you and I never disobeyed your command, yet you never gave me a young goat, that I might celebrate with my friends." (Luke 15:29)

"These many years I have served you." The word translated 'serve' refers to a bond-slave, one who is the property of his master. That word exposed the elder brother's attitude. He was thinking more like an enslaved orphan than a son. He was not serving his father out of love; he was simply obeying commands. He was bound by his own legalism.

"You never even gave me a young goat." There was a barb in his retort. The goat, as distinct from the fatted calf, would not have been appropriate for a celebration. This statement accused the father of being stingy. Like the prodigal before he came to himself, the elder brother did not see himself as the son of a good father. Will this son ever come to himself?

As long as he thought of his father as tightfisted, he would continue to work on the farm as a bond-slave, as one who has no rights. No matter how hard a bond-slave works, he still has no rights. One who is a slave in his heart can only hope for a favor from his master. Slaves cannot use the master's belongings without permission. He can only work harder and yearn for the time when his master will notice.

That is what the elder brother was doing. He had been working "these many years" longing for the time when his father/master would deem him worthy of a party with his friends. He had labored all those years with no recognition and no reward, at least not from his perspective. He felt he had to earn access to what belonged to his father. But it belonged to him as well. He thought he had to earn the right to have a party in his own house.

This reminds me of the servant who was given only one talent and buried it because he thought his master was a hard man (Matt. 25:24). Apparently, that servant thought the talent was still his master's responsibility. The master responded very graciously to the servants who took responsibility over the talents and invested them. But he responded harshly to the one who thought he was severe.

We receive from the Lord according to how we think of him.

When we measure accessibility in terms of how much we do, we always fall short. There is always more we could have done. We could have done it better, or more sincerely, or longer. More is always possible. So, we become workaholics trying to gain favor from a master who is hard to please. We seldom realize that Father is not judging us. We are judging ourselves.

But there is another element. His father had already given him the property. It was under his authority. He could have had the fatted calf anytime he wanted. It was his calf. He only needed to say the word and the servants would have prepared the party. He had not received what his father had given him. It was legally his but not practically.

Could it be that we are really sons and daughters of a loving Abba? How would that change our inner life if we really believed it? How would it change our outward life? What if Jesus was speaking the truth when he said God did not send him to condemn us? Was he only saying that to make us feel good? Or is it actually true? What if his love really does endure forever?

Pondering these questions may prepare us for the good path, but we will never come to the party till we see things differently, arise, and enter the house where the party is. We must not only agree intellectually with the proposition that Father loves us. We must experience his loving arms around us as we return to the house. Even the prodigal did not see clearly until he felt the embrace of his father on his return.

Righteousness based on works fails to bring us into an intimate relationship with Abba; it keeps us out of the party. It also makes intimacy with other workers difficult.

Prayer

Abba, melt our hearts with your love as you put your loving arms around us. Help us be like little children who welcome the hug without earning it.

Reflection Thirty-Three

Father and Friends

"Look, these many years I have served you and I never disobeyed your command, yet you never gave me a young goat, that I might celebrate with my friends." (Luke 15:29)

If there is any validity to what we have been saying—that the elder was trying to earn something that was already his and that he thought his father was a penny-pinching land owner—then we can also assume that this son would not have wanted his father in the house when he had a party with his friends. In other words, he wanted access to what his father owned but was not interested in an intimate relationship with him.

The scribes and Pharisees, the ones to whom the parable was originally addressed, were like that. As descendants of Abraham they had a favored position with the Lord of the covenant. That status came to them as a birthright, but they still thought they had to earn admiration and respect. They also were not interested in intimacy with the God they worshiped. They wanted intimacy with the Torah and kudos from their peers.

To maintain the high regard of their peers the Pharisees wore robes that marked them off from ordinary people whom they considered inferior sinners. They added certain markings to their robes that drew attention to their religious achievements. Their robes were like masks that hid the truth of who they were inside. They may have felt like they would be cast out of the elite group if anyone found out what they were really like.

The elder brother's party probably would have consisted of people masquerading as reputable members of the community. They would be wearing expensive, ostentatious robes and showy masks to avoid being seen as what they really were. Those present would not have been friends—not really. They would have been interested in the status that came with being among the few invited to such a highly esteemed farmer's house.

The prodigal had faced something similar in the foreign country. He probably had many friends as long as his money lasted. When he depleted his capital, however, none of his friends offered him food or a place to stay. Those who appeared to be friends were craving something the prodigal had. They had no interest in developing the intimacy of a true friendship with him.

True friends do things together. One initiates, the other responds and the relationship becomes a dance of intimacy. This kind of friendship is seen in the Godhead. The Father and Son were friends. "*For the Father loves [phileo] the Son and shows him all that he himself is doing*" (Jn. 5:20). Love in this text is friendship love. Father leads, Son follows, and the Father works his work through the Son, and the dance continues.

Jesus said to his disciples (to us), "*No longer do I call you servants.*" Why then do we continue to act as though we are servants? He continued, "*I have called you friends, for all that I have heard from My father I have made known to you*" (Jn. 15:15). He wants us to respond to what he makes known to us just as he responded to what Father showed him. He wants to dance with us.

Our Father wants to be our friend. Jesus said, "...the Father himself loves [phileo] you..." (Jn. 16:27). How awesome is that? The friendship Jesus had with his Father is available to us as well. Our Father does not want servants who simply obey rules, he wants a relationship with his sons and daughters. He wants to dance the life-dance with us.

Too many of us, perhaps all of us at one time or another, want access to what our Father owns rather than desiring a relationship. There is an elder brother in all of us that tries to earn access to what is already ours.

Prayer

"*Father draw us into that friendship you had with your Firstborn Son. We desire to do things with you as friend with friend.*"

Reflection Thirty-Four

Jealousy Prevents Intimacy

"But when this son of yours came, who has devoured your property withprostitutes, you killed the fattened calf for him." *(Luke 15:30)*

"This son of yours," he answered with a voice of disapproval. He did not even acknowledge that this was his brother who had returned. His breath reeks of jealousy as he speaks. The breach between him and his brother was as wide and cavernous as the one between himself and his father.

"Who devoured your property," he said. He still thought it all belonged to his father. He had not received what had been given him nor had he acknowledged that the father had released the property to the younger brother. It is true that the prodigal wasted his property. That was an affront to his father who was so generous. But it was his to waste—to his shame.

This son of yours "devoured your property with prostitutes," the elder brother said caustically. The Pharisees had demonstrated the same attitude toward Jesus just because he associated with prostitutes. Those who need to appear better than others are obliged to deride anyone who falls short of their standard. It helps them to avoid facing themselves. It also blocks intimacy.

You can almost feel the elder brother's blood boiling with the acid of bitterness. Is it possible his blood was boiling because he was secretly craving what the younger brother had experienced? Envy always has a secret desire to have what the other has. To cover his own lust, he had to be openly hostile to any who dared to do what he secretly wanted to do.

Every day the elder brother went to the field his mind was occupied with his brother's betrayal. That made him work all the harder to prove to his father he was not wasteful or profligate like little brother. The harder he worked the deeper he sank into the mire of resentment. Of course, he blamed his father and his brother for his depression.

Jesus was not ashamed to befriend those prodigals who were seeking love in all the wrong places. He had the real thing for them, the real abiding love of his Father. He knew their only hope was to find the reality to replace the counterfeit they were trying to enjoy. He knew what they were really looking for—a sense of belonging, of being at home. They would find that with him.

Sinners will never find what they are really looking for in the presence of self-righteous elder brothers. If sinners are not comfortable around us, we need to wonder what we are missing rather than blaming them. Do we give off a stench of judgment and disapproval when they are around? Do we register disgust when we see their condition? If we do, they know it. They probably know it before we do.

To be like Jesus is to be comfortable in the presence of the outcasts of society without participating in their way of life. He lived his life in total openness to both outsiders and insiders without compromising his relationship with his Father. Jesus' openness to the self-righteous religious leaders was much like the father in the prodigal story. His openness led him to confront the elder brother; but his rebuke was not from anger.

Jesus was doing as his Father showed him when his openness led him to confront the Pharisees' pride. He did not pretend approval just to be acceptable in their sight. They were not comfortable around him because he saw through their pretense. Their discomfort led them to resist him, to reject him and finally to hand him over to the Romans. Like Cain, they had to get rid of the one who exposed their imperfection.

In their pride these Pharisees may have been jealous of the popularity he enjoyed with the greater population. Rather than admit their jealousy, they put Jesus on trial to prove he was not worthy of that popularity. Their jealousy kept them from experiencing the intimacy he was offering.

Our response to a little brother or sister who returns from a life of sin will expose our heart.

Prayer

Father, help us face the exposure of our heart so we can see things differently. We desire to experience ever increasing intimacy in yourhouse.

Reflection Thirty-Five

Father's Unconditional Acceptance

"Son, you are always with me, and all that is mine is yours. It was fitting to celebrate and be glad, for this your brother was dead, and is alive; he was lost, and is found." (Luke 15:31-32)

"Son, you are always with me," the father said He called him *son*. The father accepted his son despite the son's bitterness and pride. The father held his son in his heart; but the son's heart was distant and alienated from his father. Intimacy requires of both parties a willingness to give and an openness to receive. In intimacy both give, and both receive.

The same unconditional love experienced by the returning prodigal was available to the elder brother. Love was there in his father's heart, but the son never received it. His focus was so much on the failure of others that he never even noticed he was missing a life of joy. His inner self-talk was like a raging fire against the one who loved him. He was consumed by his resentment.

To be outside the circle of true love is to be lost even if you are living on the same farm. The elder was as lost as his brother was while in the foreign country. In fact, his lost condition was more serious because he thought he was okay and everyone else was lost. God's love has been compared to rain. You might say this son's heart had a waterproof covering.

It is not enough to be loved with an everlasting love. The love is enough, but we must receive that love before we can experience its benefits. God sent the Son of his love and through him offered love to the lost world. The whole world has not yet received that love. The world's rejection of this love does not alter God. God is love, and his love remains despite our refusal to respond. His love endures forever.

We were created for intimate relationships, to reflect the image of God's loves. But intimacy is costly. You must give something of yourself to have a genuine relationship with another. Even Jesus "did not count equality with God a thing to be grasped" (Phil. 2:6). The Father gave his Son and the Son gave his life. This divine giving was all about the potential of an intimate relationship with men and women.

The goodness of the Father can have little effect on us if we are self-consumed rather than consumed by his love. Even good fathers sometimes have sons and daughters who turn away, Father God lost his first two kids—Adam and Eve. He was obviously a good and loving Father. Adam and Eve believed the enemies lie and began to think God did not really love them. If they had known his love intimately, they would never have eaten the forbidden fruit.

"All that I have is yours," the father said. When the father divided the property between his sons, he did not change his mind later. Our Father God did not change his mind either. He gave us his Son and offered even more. Paul spoke of God giving his Son, then added, "will he not also with him graciously give us all things?" (Rom. 8:32). He gave Adam (humanity) authority over all things. All Abba Father has belongs to us.

The father restored the younger brother to a full inheritance when he gave him the robe, the ring, and the sandals. All the father owned now belonged to the son who had gone astray. This is one of the amazing things about our Father's estate: all of it belongs to all of us even as it all remains his. What a wonderful sharing family we have. This love endures forever.

The father wanted intimacy with the elder son, but he also yearned for the two brothers to be reconciled to one another as well. If his love had been of a lesser quality, he could have been satisfied to have one of his sons in the house with him. He could have remained with those at the party enjoying himself. But his love would not allow him to remain in the house when one of his sons was at odds with the other. He wanted his family to be whole.

Our Father also wants a family where love flows freely. He still leaves his house to woo those who harbor bitterness in their heart toward him and toward his other children. He yearns for the unity of the Trinity to be manifest in the earth through us, his beloved children (Jn. 17).

We will never experience total intimacy until we open our heart to receive the love Abba offers and allow that love to flow to others he places in our path.

Prayer

Father, come along side us to bring us into total intimacy with you and with our fellow travelers. We will not be satisfied until we are resting in your bosom together with the other returning prodigals and field workers.

Reflection Thirty-Six

Celebration is Appropriate

"Son, you are always with me, and all that is mine is yours. It was fitting to celebrate and be glad for this your brother was dead, and is alive; he was lost, and is found." (Luke 15:31-32)

It was fitting to celebrate and be glad. Celebration and gladness go together. You cannot have one without the other. The joy and excitement itself are the first acts of celebration. The father's celebration began when he saw his younger son at a distance. His heart was already leaping for joy before he ran to meet the returning prodigal.

Joy is an automatic response to a hope realized. The party that followed, however, was much more than a formal expression of that joy. The meal was a fellowship meal honoring the returning prodigal. As in the lost sheep and lost coin parables, friends and family were invited to rejoice with the father whose hope had been realized.

It is impossible to celebrate alone. Celebration feels empty if there is no one to share the moment. When you are home alone after a victory or meaningful accomplishment, your loneliness kills the joy that is under the surface looking for someone to share the excitement.

Celebration is also stifled if you share your victory and your companion is less than enthusiastic. You need someone to listen who cares. In fact, as others respond joyfully to your story, your joy increases. Delight begets delight among those who share a common interest. If your story is met with disinterest or ridicule, your joy is quenched to some degree.

When we celebrate, we desire as many as possible to share the joy. If you have even one person who cares, your joy will increase. But there is a limit to the level of an opportunity to share the moment with as many others as possible. That is why the king in other parables wanted his banquet hall full.

The level of joy is related to the importance of the event to the ones celebrating. When the elder brother refused to rejoice, he exposed the fact that his brother's return was not important to him. In fact, he was displeased with his father who was celebrating the prodigal's return just as the Pharisees were displeased with Jesus who ate with sinners. His father's heart must have been grieved by his older son's negative response.

That is probably one of the reasons the father left the party. He knew the joy would not be complete without the whole family. People would eventually notice the older brother's absence. They would continue to be delighted in the younger son's return, but there would be a limit to their ability to give themselves completely to the celebration.

The younger brother was probably so overwhelmed by the reception that he did not notice his brother's absence at first. But sooner or later he would have noticed. When he did become aware, he would be so awed by his father's love and acceptance he would want his brother there as well. His brother's absence would have caused him to experience a degree of restraint.

That is the way it is with celebration here and now. What it will be in eternity with Abba, we can only imagine. It will be awesome because the whole family will be together in unity. But for now, our commission is to go to the highways and byways inviting strangers, older brothers, and prodigals to join us in our journey toward the bosom of the Father whose love endures forever.

Our joy is limited here and now to the degree that division invades the Church and the world. If you want more joy, invite more to join you in your journey.

Prayer

Abba Father, draw us into your bosom and send us into the world with your love. Give us boldness to invite and entreat others to join the party.

Part Seven

The Last Paragraph

The story of the prodigal ends with the announcement that the dead son was alive, the lost son was found. That announcement was addressed to the elder brother as an invitation to join the celebration. Thus, ends the final paragraph of this parable.

The last paragraph of the elder brother's life was not recorded. We do not know if he saw things differently and joined the party or continued to harbor bitterness. He may have spent more of his time and energy trying to earn that place in Father's house which was already his. Jesus may have ended the story here in the hope that the Pharisees would get the point.

Some Pharisees, like Nicodemus, did come to see things differently. There were others who kept their discipleship secret for fear of the Jews (Jn. 19:38). Their story ended on a positive note. But many of the religious leaders never came around. The last paragraph of their life was like the final act of a tragedy.

The last paragraph of the lost sheep parable ended with rejoicing. The sheep did nothing to attract the attention of the shepherd except to simply be a sheep who belonged with the shepherd. The sheep did nothing to get found. The shepherd took full responsibility for what he lost and came looking for his sheep.

The coin did nothing to get lost or to be found. The woman took full responsibility for what she lost. She lit the lamp and diligently searched until she found the missing coin. Her diligence revealed her understanding of the importance of the coin and her determination to return it to its place.

That is a picture of our Abba Father who took full responsibility for what he lost. He sent his Son as the Good Shepherd to find us. Abba did not retire from being a redeemer after he raised his Son from the dead. He continues today to be the one he has always been. He is the Father who is committed to the world despite its rejection of him.

The story of the prodigal son added to those two stories. The response of the one who was lost is not mentioned in the lost sheep or the lost coin. When personal relationships are at stake, love is what will bind us together in unity. The parable of the prodigal reveals the necessity of the beloved responding to the love offered. Father cannot coerce or control without ceasing to be love. His love can only wait for a response.

What should we do to ensure that the last paragraph of our life ends with rejoicing? First, we must acknowledge that we are the ones who belong with the shepherd—and we do. We can do nothing to get ourselves found, but we can respond when he finds us. We can simply relax on his shoulder as he returns home. He will do the rest.

The point of the lost coin is different. We, as the Bride of Christ, must take responsibility for what *we* lost—the tokens of belonging to him. Our Bridegroom gave us the Spirit as a pledge. We often neglect the gifts and lose one or more of the coins. He continues to provide a lamp, his illuminating Word, to expose what is covered in darkness and clutter. We must make use of that light to find what we lost.

Some see a difficulty when we say we must respond. There is a doctrine that says it is all up to God and nothing we can do will change what God has decided to do. The problem with that doctrine is that God, our Father, has decided to leave the decision up to us. His love is available to the whole world, but only those who respond to his love receive the benefit of that love. His challenge to us is, and always has been, "Choose you this day whom you will serve" (Josh. 24:15).

Recently I was reflecting on a helium balloon a small boy was holding. The balloon produced its own lift because of the helium. If it had been much bigger, it would have lifted the boy off the ground. Father's love is like that. It can lift us off the ground level of mediocrity into the heavenlies.

If the boy released his grip on the string, the lift would no longer be available to him. His grip did not create the lift, the balloon did. No matter how hard he might grip a string with nothing on the end of it, no lift would result. Likewise, no matter how much lifting power the balloon has, there will be no uplifting experience if there is no grip.

That is the contribution of the story of the prodigal son. The prodigal son took responsibility for his own absence from Abba's house. He 'got a grip' when he came to himself and saw things differently. He took responsibility for what he had lost. But it was the memory of his father's love and goodness that drew him back. His father's love gave him the lift. He did not know how much lift this balloon had until his father celebrated his return with a party in the house without any penance on his part.

We will not experience the full extent of Abba's love until we are finally at the party celebrating our Father's love as he celebrates our return. None of us have yet been lifted to the heights of his love. That will have to wait until the last paragraph of our life has been recorded. Even then I suspect there will be an ever-increasing revelation of his love as we continue to rise even higher.

The last paragraph of your life is not yet recorded. What will it say? Will you still be working in the field trying to earn what is already yours? Will you be watching and judging the Father and those who receive his embrace without deserving it? Will you be an uninvolved observer of those who enjoy Abba's embrace? Will you be on your way approaching the house—ever drawing near but never arriving?

If you desire to be among those who made it all the way to the party, open your heart and let Abba's love lift you up into his bosom.

His love endures forever.

Get a grip.

Acknowledgments

No one ever produces anything worthwhile without some input, practical help, and encouragement from others. Only the future will reveal whether this book is worthwhile. Even those who craft works of lesser value have others to thank for various sorts of help. I am greatly indebted to many for their input, practical help, and encouragement. Here are some of them.

My wife, Lynda, has proven herself to be a faithful helper for over 56 years. She was a great help in editing these reflections. "Thanks." She bore six children for me to practice fathering on. Now that they are grown, I finally know how to do that. "Thank you, kids."

Jack Frost opened my eyes to many aspects of Abba Father's love and the peril that comes into one's life when he or she begins to think like an orphan, living like there is no loving Father available to help. There are no direct quotes here, but many of the insights came through listening to Jack and reading his material. He has left us for a better place. He is resting in Father's bosom now. We miss him. "Thank you, Jack."

Pastor A. J. Baisch and his wife Mary, friends since 1982, have been a constant encouragement to me. He has allowed me to work out many of my ideas from his pulpit. I seem to think more clearly when I am speaking to an audience that is excited about what I am sharing. He provided that audience. He also provided me with an office, a quiet place to work. "Thanks."

There are also my many Facebook friends and former students. Their responses to my posts have helped me clarify my thinking and present the ideas more understandably. Some of their comments were like wind kindling the embers of smoldering ideas. "Thank you, thank you."

About the Author

Dr. Shults received a BA and MA in biblical studies from Eastern New Mexico University and a PhD in Hebrew Studies from the Linguistics Department at The University of Texas at Austin. He taught Bible and Theology on various college campuses for 40 years. Early in his career he lost confidence in the ability of intellectual understanding to cause any lasting change in the lives of his students. He began to pursue a relationship with Abba Father that would allow Father's love to come to those he taught.

He married Lynda Richards in 1964. They have six children and 12 grandchildren. They presently reside in Myrtle Beach, SC.

He retired from the college classroom in 2004 and began to travel and teach seminars and retreats here in the States and abroad. He is presently the founder and director of On Word Ministries.

Made in the USA
Columbia, SC
31 August 2022